Scripture Workbook:

For Personal Bible Study and Teaching the Bible

Scripture Workbook:

For Personal Bible Study and Teaching the Bible

By Gary F. Zeolla
Darkness to Light ministry
http://www.dtl.org

1stBooks - rev. 7/10/00

About the Book

This book contains twenty-two individual "Scripture Studies." Each study focuses on one general area of study. These studies enable individuals to do in-depth, topical studies of the Bible. They are also invaluable to the Bible study teacher preparing lessons for Sunday School or a home Bible study. They can be used for group studies as well.

The range of topics covered in the different studies is broad, from what the Bible teaches about itself, to what the Bible teaches about divorce and remarriage. Included in each study are hundreds of Scripture references. So there will be no lack of material from which to begin your studies.

So if you're an individual looking for an aid to improve for your own personal Bible studies, or a Bible study teacher or home group leader looking for help in preparing lessons, this book will be of great benefit.

The sources for the viewpoints promoted in these Scripture Studies are wide and varied. The ideas are taken from commentaries, study Bibles, theology books, books of various kinds, and most importantly, this writer's own personal study of the Scriptures.

The sources for the opposing views presented are publications of groups that promote the ideas and personal conversations this writer has had with members of such groups and adherents to the views.

Every effort has been made to ensure the accuracy of the Scripture references in these studies. But with the thousands of references presented, it is likely that a few "typos" have crept in. If the reader comes across a reference that does not make "sense" in the context presented, just go onto the next one. There are always plenty of verses listed for each point.

It is my hope and prayer that God uses these Scripture Studies to help the reader to:

"... grow in the grace and knowledge of our
Lord and Savior Jesus Christ.
To Him be the glory both now and forever.
Amen" (2 Peter 3:18).

Contents

Essentials of "the Faith"

Controversial Theologies

Ethics

Appendixes

Note: The order of the first ten Scripture Studies parallel the order of the articles on Darkness to Light's Confession of Faith (see Appendix #2).

Abbreviations Used in this Book

General

a - first half of verse (i.e. Gen 1:1a = first half of Gen 1:1).
b - second half of verse (i.e. Gen 1:1b = second half of Gen 1:1).
cf. - confer
cp. - compare
ct. - contrast
f - and the following verse (i.e. John 1:1f = John 1:1,2)
ff - and the following verses
Gr. - Greek
Heb. - Hebrew
LXX - Septuagint: A second-century BC, Greek translation of the Hebrew OT.
NT - New Testament
OT - Old Testament
v. - verse
vv. - verses

Bible Versions

ALT - *Analytical-Literal Translation of the Holy Bible.* Copyright © 1999, 2000 by Gary F. Zeolla of Darkness to Light ministry - http://www.dtl.org
KJV - *King James Version*
LITV - *Literal Translation of the Bible*, Copyright 1995-1999. Used by permission of the copyright holder, Jay P. Green Sr.

Bible Book Names

Old Testament:

Gen, Gn - Genesis
Exod, Ex - Exodus
Lev - Leviticus
Numb, Num - Numbers
Deut, Dt - Deuteronomy
Josh - Joshua
Judg, Jud - Judges
Ruth - Ruth
1Sam - 1Samuel
2Sam - 2Samuel
1Ki - 1Kings
2Ki - 2Kings
1Chron, 1Chr - 1Chronicles
2Chron, 2Chr - 2Chronicles
Ezra - Ezra
Neh - Nehemiah
Est - Esther
Job - Job
Ps - Psalms
Prov, Pr - Proverbs
Eccl - Ecclesiastes
Song - Song of Solomon
Isa - Isaiah
Jer - Jeremiah
Lam - Lamentations

Ezek, Ez - Ezekiel
Dan - Daniel
Hos - Hosea
Joel - Joel
Amos - Amos
Obad, Ob - Obadiah
Jon - Jonah
Mic - Micah
Nah - Nahum
Hab - Habakkuk
Zeph - Zephaniah
Hag - Haggai
Zech - Zechariah
Mal - Malachi

New Testament:

Matt, Mt - Matthew
Mark, Mk - Mark
Luke, Lk - Luke
John, Jn - John
1Jn - 1John
2Jn - 2John
3Jn - 3John
Rom - Romans
1Cor - 1Corinthians
2Cor - 2Corinthians
Gal - Galatians
Eph - Ephesians
Phil - Philippians
Col - Colossians
1Thes -1Thessalonians
2Thes - 2Thessalonians
1Tim - 1Timothy
2Tim - 2Timothy
Titus - Titus
Phlm - Philemon

Heb - Hebrews
Jam - James
1Pet - 1Peter
2Pet - 2Peter
Jude - Jude
Rev - Revelation

Essentials of "the Faith"

"Beloved, while I was very diligent to write to you concerning our common salvation, I found it necessary to write to you exhorting you to contend earnestly for the faith which was once for all delivered to the saints" (Jude 1:3).

The Scriptures on the Scriptures

Scripture Study #1

The Authority of the Scriptures

1) The Scriptures claim to be the very Words of God:

OT: Gen 15:1-4; Exod 20:1; Numb 1:1; 2Sam 23:2; Isa 6:1-8; Jer 1:1-9; 2:1; 13:1-8; 49:34f; Ezek 1:3; 3:16; 38:1; Dan 9:2 (cp. Jer 25:11f); Hos 1:1; 4:1; Joel 1:1; Amos 7:14-17; Jonah 1:1; 3:1-3; Obad 1:1; Micah 1:1; Zeph 1:1; Hag 1:1; 2:1; Zech 1:1,7; 4:6-8.

NT: Matt 5:17f; 15:3-6; 22:29-32,42-45; Acts 3:21; 4:31; 1Thes 2:13; 4:8; Heb 1:1; 2Tim 3:16f; 1Pet 1:25; 2Pet 1:20f; Rev 1:1-3,19; 2:1; 3:22.

2) The Scriptures are THE source of truth and knowledge:

OT: 2Sam 7:28; Ps 19:7f; 119:97-104,130; Isa 8:20.

NT: Luke 11:52; 24:25-27; John 5:39,46f; Acts 16:14; 17:11; 18:28; Rom 10:17; 2Tim 2:15; 3:14-17.

3) The Scriptures are verbally inspired:
    ("Verbal inspiration" means the very words of Scripture are inspired, not just the thoughts or ideas):

OT: Deut 4:2; 1Ki 8:56; Josh 21:43-45; 23:14; Prov 8:8f; 30:5f; Jer 1:9; 23:30f; 26:2.

NT: Matt 22:31f,41-45; Mark 12:35-37; John 6:63; 10:34f; 11:49-52; 12:47-50; 1Cor 4:6; Gal 3:16; Rev 22:18f.

4) The Scriptures warn not to alter its words and precepts:

OT: Deut 4:2; 12:32; Prov 8:8f; 30:5f; Jer 23:30f; 26:2.

NT: Matt 15:3-9; 1Cor 4:6; Rev 22:18f.

The Reliability of the Scriptures

1) God promised to preserve His words:

OT: Ps 12:6f; 89:34; Isa 40:8.

NT: Matt 5:18; 24:35; Luke 16:17; 1Pet 1:25.

2) The consistency of the Scriptures:

a. The OT and the NT:

The above references show the consistency of the two Testaments in their teachings about themselves. Other Scripture Studies in this book demonstrate the consistency of the two Testaments on many other topics.

b. Parallels between Jesus' and Paul's teachings:

Matt 7:1-5; Rom 2:1/ Matt 10:10; 1Cor 9:14/ Matt 19:8f; 1Cor 7:10-12/ Matt 22:21; Rom 13:7/ Matt 25:40;

4

1Cor 8:12/ Luke 22:19; 1Cor 11:23-26/ John 8:31-36; Rom 6:15-18.

c. Parallels between Peter and Paul's teachings:

1Pet 2:13f; Rom 13:1-4/ 1Pet 2:18; Eph 6:5-8/ 1Pet 2:22f; 2Cor 5:21/ 1Pet 3:1; 1Cor 7:14; Eph 5:22/ 1Pet 3:3f; 1Tim 2:9/ 1Pet 4:10; Rom 12:6-8.

3) Historic and prophetic reliability:

Many examples; but a particularly interesting one is:

Luke 10:13-15:

Jesus pronounces a "woe" upon three cites located on the Sea of Galilee (Chorazin, Bethsaida, and Capernaum). He, however, says nothing about the other major city in the area (Tiberias). Archeological evidence shows these four cities did exist at the time of Christ. The first three were destroyed by an earthquake around 400 AD and have never been rebuilt. However, Tiberias remains to this day (McDowell, pp. 309-311).

A comparison of maps in the back of most Bibles will demonstrate this phenomena. All four cities can be seen on the map for Palestine at the time of Christ, but the map of modern-day Israel shows only Tiberias.

4) Early creeds and hymns:
(Many early Christian creeds or hymns are possibly embedded within the pages of NT books. If this hypothesis is true it shows that core Christian beliefs were already written down and being memorized within a few years of the resurrection of Christ):

Luke 24:34; Rom 1:3; 4:25; 10:9; 1Cor 15:3-7; Phil 2:5-11; Col 1:15; 1Tim 2:5f; 3:16; 6:13-16; 2Tim 2:8,11-13.

5) The Scriptures and science:

(The Bible taught scientific ideas long before science "discovered" them):

a. **The universe:** Gen 1:1; Ps 102:25-27. Aristotle and other early philosophers believed the universe was eternal and unchanging. It is now known the universe had a beginning and is slowly decaying.

b. **Circumcision:** Gen 17:10-12. Due to blood clotting and pain sensitivity factors, the eighth day is the best time to perform this procedure.

c. **Sexual laws:** Exod 20:14; Lev 18:6-23; Deut 28:1-5,15f,27f,58-61. The Scriptures link disobedience to the Law of God, which includes prohibitions on sexual sin, with the contracting of disease.

d. **Sanitation laws:** Lev 6:28; 14:2-9; 17:13; Numb 5:2f; 19:11; Deut 23:12f. Basic sanitary procedures today but generally unknown at the time.

e. **Dietary laws:** Lev 7:22-27; 11:1-47. Restrictions on the eating of certain kinds of meat and on animal fat, which are now known to cause health problems.

f. **The earth:** Job 26:7. Many religions during Biblical times taught the earth was "sitting" on something.

g. **Ocean currents:** Job 38:16; Ps 8:8; Isa 43:16: The presence of such currents was not confirmed until the fifteenth century.

h. **The shape of the earth:** Ps 103:12: One can only travel east or west indefinitely if the earth is round. Luke 17:31-37: The only way Jesus can return "in that day" and "in that night" at the same time is if the earth is round (see also Isa 40:22).

i. **The origin of rainfall:** Ps 135:7; Eccl 1:7; Amos 5:8. Simple, but accurate descriptions of the water cycle.

j. **The number stars = sands of the seas** (i.e. are uncountable): Gen 15:5; 22:17; 32:12; cp. Gen 49:49. Only approximately 3000 stars are visible with the naked eye. With the use of the telescope we now know there are billions and billions of stars, just as there are billions and billions of grains of sand on the earth.

The Finality of the Scriptures

Is God still giving special revelation today?

Yes (answer of Mormons and other groups whose leaders claim to be "prophets"):

Amos 3:7:
God always has prophets to reveal "His secret" to.

BUT: This verse states what God does when there are prophets like Amos. It doesn't follow there must always be such prophets (see Numb 12:6).

1Cor 12:10; Acts 2:17f:
Certain people have the gift of prophecy.

BUT: The type of prophecy referred to is one of "edification and exhortation and comfort" (1Cor 14:3). These functions can be performed by people without the "gift of prophecy" (2Cor 1:3f; Eph 4:29; Heb 3:12f). The words of these kinds of prophets did not have the authority of Scripture.

No (answer of historic Christianity):

Acts 20:27; 2Tim 3:16f:
We already have "the whole counsel of God" and all we need to be "thoroughly equipped." So any further revelation would be either redundant or would have to conflict with what has already been revealed (but see Deut 13:1-3; 18:20-22; Gal 1:6-9).

Jude 3:
Jude mentions "the faith which was once for all delivered to the saints." He gives us no hint we should be looking forward to further elements of "the faith" to be revealed.

Heb 1:1f:
Christ is God's final Word to us.

2Pet 1:12-15; 3:1:
Peter's concern is that believers always remember what has already been revealed. He doesn't tell us to be looking for further revelation from God.

Studying the Scriptures

1) Topical study:
(Glean information on one particular issue from all parts of the Bible)

Luke 24:25-27; Acts 7:1-53; Rom 3:9-20; 4:1-25; 5:12-21; 9:1-11:36; 15:7-13; Gal 3:1-29; Heb 1:1-14.

Advantages:
1) One issue can be studied in depth.
2) Scripture can be used to interpret Scripture.

Disadvantage:
Tendency to only study topics one likes while ignoring many other important subjects.

2) Expository study:

(Verse by verse study through the whole Bible or a particular book or passage of the Bible).

Neh 8:1-8; Dan 9:1f; Luke 4:16-21; Acts 8:26-25.

Advantages:
1) Will cover a wide range of topics.
2) Forced to deal with whatever topics come up.

Disadvantage:
Danger of basing a doctrine or practice on one passage of Scripture.

Suggestion:
Both forms of study should be utilized to counter-balance the advantages and disadvantages of each. Perhaps an expository daily Bible reading program with topical studies, such as those in this book, as time allows.

Bibliography: Some of the information for "The Scriptures and Science" section was gleaned from:

Barfield, Kenny. *Why the Bible is Number 1*. Grand Rapids: Baker Book House, 1988.
Also: McDowell, Josh. *Evidence that Demands a Verdict*. San Bernardino, CA: Here's Life Publishers, 1979.

All Scripture references from: *The New King James Version*. Nashville, TN: Thomas Nelson Publishers, 1982, unless otherwise indicated.

The Attributes of God

Scripture Study #2

1) Personal:
(God is a self-conscious Being capable of thought, will, and interaction with others.)

OT: Gen 1:1-31; Exod 20:1-17; Job 12:13; Ps 2:4; Prov 3:19f; Isa 55:8f.

NT: Matt 6:1-15; 2Cor 1:3f; 1Thes 4:3,7.

2) Creator:
(All of creation came into existence through the will and power of God.)

OT: Gen 1:1-31; Neh 9:5f; Job 38:1-41; Ps 19:1; 24:1f; 33:6-9; 89:11f; 95:6f; 102:25-27; Isa 44:24; 45:18; Zech 12:1.

NT: Acts 14:15; Rom 1:20; Heb 11:3; Rev 4:11.

3) Live Giver:
(All life was created by and is dependent on God.)

OT: Gen 2:7; Ps 36:9; Job 12:10; 33:3; Dan 5:23.

NT: Acts 17:25; 1Tim 6:13; Rev 22:1.

4) Spirit/ Invisible:
(God's existence is immaterial, non-physical, and distinct from His creation.)

OT: Exod 20:4; Dt 4:11; Job 9:11; 23:8f; 35:14.

NT: John 1:18; 4:24 (cp. Luke 24:39); 6:46; Col 1:15; 1Tim 1:17; 6:16; Heb 11:27; 1John 4:12.

5) Omnipresent:
(All of God is present in all places at all times.)

OT: 1Sam 2:3; 1Ki 8:27; Ps 73:23-28; 139:7f; Jer 23:23f.

NT: John 4:20-24; Acts 7:48-50; 17:26-28; Eph 4:6; Heb 13:5f.

6) Omniscient:
(God knows all things knowable.)

OT: 1Ki 8:37-39; Job 34:21f; 37:16; 38:1-3; Ps 10:11-15; 33:13-15; 59:5-9; 94:4-11; 139:1-6,11f,15-18; 147:4f; Prov 15:3; Eccl 12:13f; Isa 29:15f; 40:12-14,25-28; Jer 16:17; 32:19; Zech 4:10.

NT: Matt 6:7f; 10:30; Acts 15:18; Rom 11:33; Col 2:3; Heb 4:13; 1John 3:20.

7) Knows the Future:
(God's omniscience includes knowledge of all that will come to pass before it occurs.)

OT: Gen 15:13f; Exod 3:19; Deut 31:15-21; 1Ki 13:1f (see 2Ki 23:15f); 1Ki 14:12f,17f; Josh 6:2 (see 1Ki 16:34); Ps 139:4, 16; Isa 40:12-14,27-31; 41:21-24; 44:6-8; 48:3-5; 65:24; Jer 1:5; 32:3-5 (cp. Ezek 12:13; 2Ki 25:5-7); Dan 2:28.

NT: Matt 2:4-6; Eph 1:3f; Acts 3:18; 15:16-18; 1Cor 15:3f; Rev 13:8; 17:8.

8) Omnipotent:
(God can do all things capable of being done with an unlimited amount of power.)

OT: Gen 17:1; 18:14; Deut 32:39; 2Chr 20:6; Ps 33:6-11; 115:3; 135:6; Isa 14:24-27; 40:28; 43:13; Jer 32:17,27.

NT: Matt 19:26; Luke 1:37; 18:27; Rom 8:31; Rev 19:6.

9) Sovereign:
(God is absolute Lord over His creation and all that occurs therein.)

OT: 1Sam 2:6-10; Lam 3:37-39; Job 9:12 (cp. 23:1-7); 34:24-30; 36:22f; 37:20; 38:1-4; 40:1-8; 42:1-6; Ps 2:1-12; 33:10f; 37:12f; 103:19; 135:6f; Isa 40:12-17,22f; 45:9f; 64:8: Dan 4:35.

NT: Matt 10:29; Acts 5:38f; 17:24-26; 18:9f; Rom 9:20; Jam 4:13-15.

10) Incomprehensible:
(God cannot be fully known.)

OT: Job 9:10; 11:7-9; 36:26; Ps 139:6; 145:3; Isa 40:28; 55:8f.

NT: Rom 11:33-36; 1Cor 2:11,16; Eph 3:9; Phil 4:7.

But God can be known truly: Jer 9:23f; Dan 11:32; John 17:3; 1Cor 13:9-12; Eph 1:9; 1John 5:20.

11) Eternal:
(God had no beginning and will have no end.)

OT: Gen 1:1; 21:33; Exod 3:14; Deut 32:40; 33:27; Job 36:26; Ps 10:16; 41:13; 90:2; 93:2; 102:27; 106:48; 117:1f; Isa 40:28; 43:13; 44:6; 57:15; Hab 1:12.

NT: Acts 15:18; Rom 1:20; 16:25f; 1Tim 1:17; 6:16; Heb 4:3; 11:3; Rev 1:4; 11:17; 21:6.

12) Self-Existent:
(God has life within Himself; His existence is not dependent upon any other.)

OT: Gen 1:1; Exod 3:14.

NT: John 5:26; Acts 17:24f; 1Tim 1:17; 6:16.

13) Immutable:
(God does not change in His nature, character, or dependability.)

OT: Gen 8:22; 9:8-13; Numb 23:19; 1Sam 15:29; Lam 3:22f; Ps 33:1; 89:34; 102:24-27; Isa 40:28; Mal 3:6.

NT: Rom 11:29; 2Tim 2:11-13; Titus 1:1-3; Heb 6:13-20; 10:19-23; Jam 1:17.

14) Perfect:
(God is flawless and complete. He does not lack anything, nor does He have any moral imperfection.)

OT: Gen 18:14; Deut 3:3f; 2Sam 22:31-33; Job 21:22; Ps 19:7.

NT: Matt 5:48; Rom 12:2; 1John 3:3.

15) Incomparable:
(God is superior over all things in His essence, character, and actions, and He is worthy of all praise.)

OT: Exod 15:11; Deut 33:26; 2Sam 7:22; Ps 35:10; 50:21; 71:19; 86:8-10; 97:9; 113:4-6; Isa 40:25; Jer 10:6-16.

NT: 1Tim 1:17; 6:15f; Jude 25; Rev 4:8-11.

16) Good:
(The moral character of God.)

OT: Exod 34:6; 1Chr 16:34; Ps 25:8; 34:8-10; 135:3; Lam 3:25; Nahum 1:7.

NT: Matt 7:11; Acts 14:17; Rom 2:4; 2Thes 1:11.

17) Holy:
(God is separate from all else, especially from all evil.)

OT: Exod 3:5; 19:10-21: 20:18-21; 33:18-23; Lev 19:2; Deut 5:23-27; 1Sam 2:2; 6:20; Ps 22:3; Isa 6:1-5; 57:15; Jer 5:22; Hab 2:20.

NT: Jam 1:13; 1Pet 1:15f; Rev 3:7; 4:8-10; 15:3f.

18) Righteous and Just:
(God's nature and actions are always morally right.)

OT: Gen 18:25; Exod 9:27; Ps 11:7; 19:8f; 33:4f; 89:14; 97:2-6; 111:3; 119:142,160,172; 129:4.

NT: Matt 6:33; Acts 17:30f; Rom 1:16f; 3:21-26; 3:21-26; 7:12; Jam 1:13; 1John 1:5,9; 3:7; Rev 15:3; 16:4-7; 19:2.

19) Judge:
(God is the final determiner of what is morally right or wrong; all people are answerable to Him and His standards.)

OT: Gen 18:25; Deut 32:34-43; 1Sam 2:3,10; 1Chr 16:33; Ps 7:11; 9:7f; 10:8-18; 10:8-18; 50:1-6; 58:10f; 82:8; 94:2; 96:13; 98:9; Isa 66:14-17.

NT: Rom 1:32; 2:2-5; 10:16; Heb 10:30; 12:23; 13:4; Rev 20:11-15.

20) Wrath:
(God's moral character leads Him to judge and punish all unrighteousness.)

OT: Exod 15:7-10; 22:22-24; Deut 4:24; 7:10; 32:21f; Isa 13:11-13; Jer 10:10.

NT: Matt 3:7; Luke 12:2-5; John 3:36; Rom 1:18; 2:5; 5:9; Eph 2:3; Col 3:6; 5:6; 1Thes 1:10; Heb 10:26-31; 12:29; Rev 11:16-19; 15:1,7f; 16:1.

Immediate judgments: Gen 38:7-10; Lev 10:1-3 (cp. 16:13); Numb 16:1-49; 21:4-9; 2Sam 6:1-13; Ezek 18:4; Luke 13:1-5; Acts 5:1-11; 12:20-23 (cp. Gen 2:16f; 3:1-6; 5:5).

21) Grace, Mercy, and Love:
(God's dealings with His people are based on His goodness, generosity, concern, and compassion, instead of on what we deserve.)

OT: Deut 7:7-9; 10:15-18; 33:12; 1Chr 16:34; Neh 9:17; Ps 63:3; 86:15; 100:5; 103:8; 119:64; 145:8f; Isa 63:7-9; Jer 31:3; Lam 3:22-26; Dan 9:9; Jonah 3:10-4:2.

NT: John 3:16; Rom 5:8-11; Eph 1:6f; 2:4-10; Titus 3:3-7; 1John 4:9f; 5:11-13; Rev 21:4.

Opposing Views

1) God is Finite (i.e. not omnipresent; Mormons, Jehovah's Witnesses):

1Ki 8:39; Ps 33:13f; Matt 6:9: God is in heaven; He cannot be everywhere.

BUT: In 1Kings 8, in addition to saying God's dwelling place is in heaven (v.39), Solomon also says God will be in the temple he had just built on earth (v.13). So Solomon clearly believed God could be in more than one place at a time. In fact, He is bigger than heaven and earth! (v.27).

When the Bible declares God "dwells" somewhere it is not restricting Him to that place. It is proclaiming that God is MANIFESTING Himself at that time in that place (see 1Sam 4:4; Numb 7:89; Ps 80:1; 99:1: Isa 57:15; 1Cor 3:16; 2Cor 6:16). The spiritual world is always present, but we do not always see it unless allowed to by God (2Ki 6:15-17; Exod 40:34; Numb 22:31; 1Ki 8:10f; Luke 2:13f; Acts 7:55; Rev 4:2-5).

2) God has a physical body (Mormons):
Gen 1:26; Isa 37:17; 45:12; 51:5; 60:13: We are created in the image of God's physical body.

BUT: The Bible also says God has wings--but we don't! (Ruth 2:12; Ps 17:8; 36:7; 91:4; 98:8). Ascribing physical characteristics to God is done to aid our finite minds in understanding God's infinite nature. For example, God's "arms" indicate his power and care for us (Isa 40:10-12); His "wings" show the tenderness of this care (see Matt 23:37).

Also, taking descriptions of God's "physical body" literally would lead to some ridiculous conclusions (see 2Chr 16:9; Prov 15:3; Zech 4:10). The image of God in people consists of immaterial qualities (Eph 4:24; Col 3:10).

3) God is not omniscient (Process theology):
Gen 3:8f; 11:5; 22:12; Numb 22:9; Job 1:7; 2:2: God needs to ask questions, so He cannot be all-knowing.

BUT: God asks questions like these not for His benefit but to confront us about our sins (Job 38:1-3; 42:5f).

4) God is mutable (Process Theology):
Gen 6:6; Exod 32:14; 1Sam 15:11,35; Jonah 1:1f; 3:4-10: God changes His mind, so He is not immutable.

BUT: God's eternal, unchanging nature is to judge sin and forgive those who repent (Deut 7:9f; Jer 3:12f; Jonah 4:11).

Bibliography:
Some of the above definitions are adapted from pages 64-68 of Erickson, Millard. *Concise Dictionary of Christian Theology*. Grand Rapids: Baker Book House, 1986.

All Scripture references from: *New King James Version*. Nashville, TN: Thomas Nelson Publishers, 1982, unless otherwise indicated.

The Attributes of God: Scripture Study. Contained in the book *Scripture Workbook*. Copyright © 1999-2000 by Gary F. Zeolla of Darkness to Light ministry - http://www.dtl.org

The Doctrine of the Trinity:

God's Three-in-Oneness

Scripture Study #3

I)   There is only one true God:

OT: Exod 8:10; Deut 4:35; 6:4; 2Sam 7:22; 1Ki 8:60; Neh 9:6; Ps 18:31; Isa 43:10; 44:6,8; 45:5f,14,18,21; 46:9

NT: John 5:44; 17:3; 1Cor 8:4-5; 1Tim 2:5.

II)   The Father is God:

OT: Deut 32:6; Ps 89:26; Isa 63:16; 64:8; Mal 1:6; 2:10

NT: Matt 6:9; John 6:27; Gal 1:1-3; Eph 4:6; 5:20; 6:23; Phil 2:11; 4:20; Col 3:17; Jude 1.

III)   The Son is God:

1) Called God or Ascribed Deity:

OT: Gen 19:24; Ps 45:7; Isa 7:14; 9:6; Jer 23:5f; Zech 2:10-3:2; 12:10

NT: Matt 1:22f; John 1:1; 5:18; 20:28; Acts 20:28; Rom 8:9; 9:5; Phil 2:5-9; Col 2:9; 1Tim 3:16; Titus 2:13; Heb 1:3,8f; 2Pet 1:1; 1John 5:20.

2) Spoke and Acted as God:

Omnipresent: Matt 18:20; 28:20; John 1:48; 3:13.

19

Omniscient: Matt 11:27; 12:25; Mark 2:8; Luke 9:46; 11:17; John 4:16-18.
Foretold the future: Matt 16:21; 24:18f,25; 26:21-25,31-35; Mark 14:30; John 6:64,70f; 21:18f (cp. Isa 41:21-23).
Omnipotent: Rev 1:8; 3:7.
Sovereign: Matt 17:24-27; 28:18.
Controlled the weather: Matt 14:32; Mark 4:39-41 (cp. Job 38:25-38; Ps 135:7).
Incomprehensible: Matt 11:27.
Holy: Josh 5:13-15 (cp. Exod 3:5f); John 8:46.
Gave commandments: Matt 5:27f,31f.
Forgave sin: Mark 2:5-11; Luke 7:47.
Love: Matt 20:28; John 15:13.

3) Ascribed Attributes of God:

Omnipresent: Eph 1:22f; 4:10.
Omniscient: John 2:23-25; 16:30; 21:17.
Omnipotent: Phil 3:20f.
Sovereign: Acts 10:36.
Eternal: Isa 9:6; Mic 5:2; John 1:1; 17:5,24; Col 1:17; Heb 7:3.
Immutable: Heb 1:8-12; 13:8.
Preeminent: Col 1:18 (cp. Ps 97:9; 148:13).
Good: John 7:12.
Holy: Matt 26:59f; Mark 4:36-41; Luke 5:1-11; 2Cor 5:21; Heb 4:15; 7:26; Rev 1:17.
Righteous: Luke 23:47; 2Cor 5:21; 1John 2:1.
Just: Zech 9:9.
Wrath: Rev 6:15-17 (cp. 11:17f).
Grace, Mercy, and Love: Matt 9:36; 14:14; John 13:1; 1Thes 5:28.

4) Does Acts of God:

Creates and Sustains: Gen 1:1; Isa 44:24; John 44:24; John 1:13; Col 1:16f; Heb 1:2f.

Gives life: Gen 2:7; 1Tim 6:13; John 1:4; 5:21; 11:25; Acts 3:15.
Judges: Ps 96:13; John 5:22f; 2Tim 4:1; Heb 13:4.
Redeems: Ps 130:7f; Isa 43:25; 44:22; Eph 1:7; Titus Heb 9:12-15; 1Pet 1:18f.
Saves: Isa 45:22; Acts 2:21; 4:12; 16:30f; 1Tim 1:15; Heb 12:2.
Fills the hungry soul: Ps 107:9; John 6:48-51.
Calms the storm: Ps 107:29; Matt 8:26.

5) Treated Like God:

Worshipped: Josh 5:13-15; Matt 14:33; 28:9,17; John 9:38; Phil 2:10f; Heb 1:6; 2Peter 3:18; Rev 5:8-14 (ct. Acts 12:20-23; 14:8-15; Rev 19:10).
Receives Divine service: Rev 22:3f (cp. Exod 20:3-5; Matt 4:10).
Prayed to: Acts 7:59f; 2Cor 12:8; 1John 5:13-15.

6) Theophanies = Christophanies:
(Appearances of God in the OT are actually appearances of Christ.)

John 1:18; 6:46; 12:41; Isa 6:1-8; Josh 5:13-6:2 (cp. Numb 13:1f).

7) The Angel of the LORD and the LORD:

Distinct persons:
2Sam 24:16f; 1Chr 21:15f,27; Zech 1:12.

Same Person:
Gen 22:1f,11f,15f; 28:10-22; 31:11-13; 48:15f (Note: "bless" is singular).
Exod 3:2,4/ Exod 13:21; 14:19.
Exod 20:1; Deut 1:6-8; Judg 2:1.
Judg 6:12-15/ Judg 13:21f.

21

8) God and the Lamb:
(Distinct, yet the same)

Rev 7:10,17; 21:22f; 22:1,3 (cp. Isa 60:19f).

9) Titles of Deity:

The Alpha and the Omega; The First and the Last: Isa 44:6; Rev 1:8,11,17f; 2:8; 21:6; 22:12-17.
King of kings; Lords of lords: Deut 10:17; Ps 136:3; 1Tim 6:15; Rev 17:14; 19:16.
Rock: Deut 2:7; 32:3d; 1Cor 10:4.
I AM: Exod 3:14; Deut 32:39; Isa 43:10; Hos 13:4; Joel 2:27; Matt 14:27; Mark 6:50; John 8:24,58 (Note: "It is I" or similar phrases in these verses are "I am" in the original languages.)
Judge: Ps 94:2; 2Tim 4:8; Heb 12;23; Jam 5:9.
Savior: Isa 43:11; Hos 13:4; 1Tim 1:1; 2:3; 2Tim 1:10; Titus 1:3f; 2:10,13f; 3:4,6.
Shepherd: Ps 23:1; Ezek 34:11-16; John 10:11,14; Heb 13:20; Rev 7:17.
Majestic: Luke 9:43; 2Pet 1:16.

10) OT Passages in NT:
(Passages in the OT referring to God are quoted in the NT as referring to the Son.)

Deut 10:14; Acts 10:36.
Ps 8:2; Matt 21:26.
Ps 34:8; 1Pet 2:3.
Ps 102:25-27; Heb 1:10f.
Ps 130:8; Matt 1:21.
Isa 26:19; 60:1; Eph 5:14.
Isa 43:10; Acts 1:8.
Isa 45:23; Phil 2:10.
Jer 2:13; 17:13; John 4:13f; 7:35-37.

Jer 9:24; 2Cor 10:17.
Jer 17:10; Rev 2:23.
Joel 2:32; Rom 10:13.
Mal 3:1; Mark 1:2.

IV)   The Holy Spirit is a Person:
(A self-conscious Being capable of thought, will, and interaction with others.)

1) Acts 13:1-5:

Speaks, commands, and calls: verse 2.
Refers to Himself with personal pronouns: "to Me" and "I" - verse 2.
Sends out missionaries: verse 4.

2) Elsewhere in the Book of Acts:

Inspired Scripture: 1:16.
Is lied to: 5:3.
Bears witness: 5:32.
Instructs: 8:29.
Comforts: 9:31.
Tells and sends: 10:19f; 11:12.
Confirms: 15:28.
Forbids: 16:6f.
Testifies: 20:23.
Makes overseers: 20:28.
Prophesies: 28:25.

3) Elsewhere in the Bible:

Hovers: Gen 1:2 (cp. Deut 32:11).
Sends: Isa 48:16.
Speaks for believers: Matt 10:16-20.
Teaches: Luke 12:12.
Assures, leads, bears witness, and enables: Rom 8:14-

17.
Loves: Rom 15:30.
Searches: 1Cor 2:10f.
Wills: 1Cor 12:11.
Fellowships: 2Cor 13:14; Phil 2:1.
Grieves: Eph 4:30.
Instructs: 1Tim 4:1.
Witnesses: Heb 10:15-18.
Is insulted: Heb 10:29.
Commands: Rev 22:17.

4) John 14:26; 15:26; 16:8,13f:

A masculine pronoun ("He" Greek: *ekeinos*, literal "that One") is applied to the Holy Spirit despite the fact that "Spirit" (Greek: *pneuma*) is neuter.

5) John 14:16:

The Spirit is "another Helper" (Greek: *allos parakletos*) besides Jesus (1John 2:1, "Advocate" in Greek is *parakletos*). See also Rom 8:26f,34.

V) The Holy Spirit is God:

1) Equated with God:

Exod 29:45f; Haggai 2:5.
Acts 5:3,4.
Rom 5:5; 2Thes 3:5.
1Cor 12:6,11,18.
2Cor 3:17.

2) The Temple of God = The Temple of the Holy Spirit:

1Cor 3:16; 6:19; 2Cor 6:16; Eph 3:19; 5:18.

24

3) Possesses Attributes of God:

Omnipresent: Ps 139:7-10.
Omniscient: 1Cor 2:10f.
Foretells the future: Acts 1:16; 20:22f; 21:33.
Omnipotent: Luke 1:35-37.
Eternal: Heb 9:14.
Good: Ps 143:10.
Holy: Rom 1:4.
Grace: Zech 12:10; Heb 10:29.

4) Does the Works of God:

Creates: Job 26:13.
Forms humans: Gen 2:7; Job 33:4.
Calls into ministry: Matt 9:38; Acts 13:2; 20:28.
Inspired Scripture: 2Tim 3:16; 2Pet 1:20f; Rev 1:1; 2:7.
Gives eternal life: John 3:3-8; Titus 3:5; 1John 5:11.

5) The Spirit's Words are Equated with God's Words:

Lev 16:1-34; Heb 9:7f.
Isa 6:9f; Acts 28:25-27.
Jer 31:33f; Heb 10:15f.

VI) The Father, the Son, and the Spirit are distinct from each other:

1) In the OT:

Gen 1:2,26f; 11:7; Neh 9:20; Ps 2:1-9; Prov 30:4; Isa 6:8; 48:16; 63:11.

2) In the Gospels:

Matt 3:16; 4:1,6; 11:25-27; 12:32f; 14:23; 16:16f; 17:5; 26:39; 27:46; 28:18f.
Mark 1:1,8; 13:32; 15:34.
Luke 2:49; 4:18; 6:12; 11:13; 23:34,46.
John 1:1f; 3:16f; 5:19f,30; 6:27,37-46; 8:17f; 11:41f; 13:1; 14:6,16,26; 15:26; 16:13f; 17:1,24; 20:17,21f,30f.

3) In the Book of Acts:

2:22-36; 3:13-15; 4:24-30; 7:55f; 10:34-42; 13:33-37; 15:8; 17:30f; 20:21.

4) Elsewhere in the NT:

Rom 1:1-9; 1Cor 1:1-9; 2:10f; 2Cor 5:18-21; 13:14; Gal 4:4-6; Eph 2:18; Phil 2:5-11; Col 2:2; 1Thes 4:8; Heb 1:1-8; 2:17; 5:5-10; 7:25; 9:14; 1John 1:3; 2John 3; Jude 1; Rev 1:1-6.

Summary:

The Bible teaches God is in some way "three" and in some way "one." So God is a "tri-unity" or more simply "Trinity." And the doctrine of the Trinity is an attempt to explain God's three-in-oneness without ending up in a logical contradiction. A simple statement of this doctrine is, "God is three Persons in one essence." Or more fully:

"Within the one Being or essence of God, there eternally exist three distinct yet equal Persons, God the Father, God the Son and God the Holy Spirit" (Article #3 on Darkness to Light's Confession of Faith, see Appendix #2).

Note: All Scripture references from: *The New King James Version*. Nashville, TN: Thomas Nelson Publishers, 1982, unless otherwise indicated.

Arguments Against the Trinity

With Rebuttals

Scripture Study #4

Note: In this study, the "argument against the Trinity" is presented immediately below the Scripture reference. After the "BUT" is the rebuttal to the argument.

Arguments Against Trinity "Proof-Texts"

Psalm 102:25-27:
Application of this passage to Jesus in Heb 1:10-12 doesn't mean Jesus is the Creator but only the One through whom God created (Heb 1:3).

BUT: In Isaiah 44:24 God says He creates "all alone" and "by Myself."

Isaiah 7:14; Matt 1:22f:
Jesus being called "Immanuel" (God with us) doesn't mean He is God since others have names with "God" in them (e.g. Ezekiel means "God strengthens").

BUT: Jesus is never actually called Immanuel. It is not a title but a description (see also Jer 23:5f; cp. Zech 2:10).

Isaiah 9:6:
Jesus is called "Mighty God" but not "Almighty God." Thus He is not equal to the Father.

BUT: The Father is called "Mighty God" in Isa 10:21 and Jer 32:17. Further, only the Father and Son are ever given this title. And see the discussion on Rev 1:8 below.

Matthew 14:23:

When Jesus prays it does not indicate He is a distinct Person from God. Jesus' divine nature is praying to His human nature.

BUT: How does a "nature" talk to a "nature?" People talk to people. In this case, Jesus (the second Person of the Trinity) is communing with the Father (the first Person of the Trinity). See Matt 26:42.

John 1:1:

The phrase, "the Word was with God" does not mean the Son and the Father are distinct. "Word" (Gr. *logos*) simply means "something said" and refers to God's speaking in creation ("In the beginning" - cp. Gen 1:1,3).

BUT: The word "with" (Gr. *pros*) means "to, towards" when used with the accusative as it is here (Thayer, p.541). The word is generally translated "to" or "toward" (NKJV) or "unto" (KJV; see John 1:29,42,47; 2:3; 3:2,4,20,26). So this phrase cannot be referring to "something said" coming FROM God.

Also, in the first phrase of this verse "was" (Gr. *ev*) is imperfect. This verbal form indicates the Word was existing before creation began (Rienecker, p.217). So it cannot refer to "something said" during the creation period.

Lastly, logos has a wide variety of meanings in the NT. The exact meaning is determined by context. Given the above, plus the use of the definitive article ("the"), something more than just "something said" is being referred to.

John 1:1:
The second "God" doesn't have the definite article ("the"). So it must be rendered "a god."

BUT: "God" in John 1:6,12,13 doesn't have the article, but it is not rendered "a god" in these verses. The grammar is, "... emphasizing quality, the Word had the same nature as God" (Rienecker, p.217).

John 5:18:
Jesus isn't claiming Deity here; the Jews misunderstood Him.

BUT: Read the verse without the parenthetical statement about the Sabbath, "Therefore the Jews sought all the more to kill Him, because He ... said God was His own Father making Himself equal to God."

John 8:58:
"I Am" should be rendered, "I have been." And in Exod 3:14 (in the LXX) the text actually reads, "I Am the Being" not just "I Am."

BUT: "I have been" (which would be perfect tense) is an impossible rendering of the PRESENT tense verb. Also, in Deut 32:39 and Isa 43:10 God refers to Himself simply as "I Am."

John 10:30:
"I and the Father are one" only indicates they are one in agreement or purpose, not essence (cp. John 17:20-23).

BUT: Possible but not necessary interpretation.

John 20:28:
Thomas' saying "my Lord and my God" is simply an exclamation.

BUT: The text specifically reads Thomas, "said to Him" (i.e. Jesus). And, in a Jewish society, it would be blasphemy to use the words "Lord" and "God" in an exclamation.

Acts 13:1-5:
When the Holy Spirit is referred to in personal terms it is only personification.

BUT: Personification is poetic language. It is often used in poetry and personal conversations, but not in historical accounts. See also Acts 1:16; 5:3,32; 8:28; 9:31; 10:19; 11:12; 15:28; 16:6f; 20:23,28; 21:11. This is a lot of poetry in a history book!

1Timothy 6:15; Revelation 17:14; 19:16:
In Dan 2:37 Nebuchadnezzar is called "king of kings." So Jesus and God both being called by this title doesn't mean Jesus is God.

BUT: Nebuchadnezzar is not AFFIRMED as being the king of kings (see Dan 4:28-35). And by definition, there can be only one "King of kings."

Titus 2:13; 2Peter 1:1:
"God" and "Savior" refer to two different Persons, not just to Jesus.

BUT: In 2Peter 1:11; 2:20; 3:1,18 "Lord" and "Savior" both refer to Jesus and the grammatical construction is identical except "Lord" is substituted for "God."

Revelation 1:18:
The Father is speaking.

BUT: 1:7,11-18 demonstrates Jesus is speaking. This is why most "red-letter" Bibles have these words in red. Thus, it is Jesus who is calling Himself, "the Alpha and Omega" and "the Almighty" (cp. Rev 21:5-7).

Arguments Against Jesus' Deity

Proverbs 8:22:
Jesus is the "wisdom" referred to and is said to be "created."

BUT: In Proverbs chapters 1-9, "Wisdom" is being personified as a WOMAN. Thus, this cannot be a reference to the SON of God (cp. Ps 2:7; Prov 30:4).

Mark 13:32:
Jesus is not omniscient, so He cannot be God.

BUT: Ignorance and error are two different things. Also, at times Jesus spoke as being omniscient (Matt 17:27; Mark 2:8; Luke 9:46f; 11:17; John 4:16-18). He even predicted the future (Matt 16:21; 24:45; 26:21-25,31-45; John 21:18f).

Further, Christian doctrine says Jesus is full God AND full man, so He could have been speaking from His humanity (Heb 2:17). And the "kenosis" ("emptying") of the Son must always be remembered (Phil 2:6f).

Matthew 28:18:
Jesus had to receive His authority "in heaven and in earth."

BUT: After His resurrection, Jesus had His authority RESTORED to Him which He willingly "emptied Himself" of for the incarnation (Phil 2:7).

33

Luke 22:42:

Jesus prays to the Father and submits His will to the Father's. Thus, Jesus is separate from, and inferior to the Father.

BUT: The Trinity doctrine includes the idea of the Father and the Son being separate Persons with separate wills. And it is not a denial of essential equality for one person to submit to another. If it is, then women would be essentially inferior to men (Eph 5:22; but see Gal 3:28).

John 1:2:

Jesus can't be "with God" and be God.

BUT: Jesus is "with" God as regards His Person; He is equal to God the Father as regards His essence. The distinction between "Person" and "essence" must always be remembered when discussing the Trinity. The doctrine teaches God is "three Persons in one essence."

John 1:18:

"No man has seen God at any time" but people have seen Jesus.

BUT: People HAVE seen God (Gen 18; Exod 24:9-11; 33:11,20). It is God the Father no one has seen (John 6:46). The OT appearances of God are more specifically appearances of God the Son (cp. John 12:41 with Isa 6:5).

John 14:28:

Jesus states, "My Father is greater than I."

BUT: Indicates positional, not essential relationship. Or, Jesus is speaking from His human nature. Or, the result of the kenosis (Phil 2:8).

John 17:3:

The Father is "the only true God" so Jesus can't be God.

BUT: The purpose of this statement was to deny polytheism, not to teach about Jesus' essential relationship to the Father. Note Jesus' statement in verse two about receiving "authority over all flesh." This all encompassing authority the Father could not give if He had rival gods (cp. 1Cor 8:4-6, and see comments on Matt 28:18).

Further, "The very juxtaposition here of JESUS CHRIST with THE FATHER is a proof, by implication, of our Lord's Godhead. The knowledge of GOD AND A CREATURE could not be eternal life, and such an association of the one with the other would be inconceivable" (Henry Alford, quoted in Jamieson, p.1064; emphases in original; see Job 22:21; Isa 45:22; Joel 2:32; Acts 2:21, cp. Acts 4:12).

John 20:17:

Jesus calls the Father "My God" so He can't be God Himself.

BUT: This is an indication of the positional difference between the Father and the Son. Compare Genesis 18:12 where Sarah called Abraham "Lord" (Heb. adonai). But by referring to her husband in this manner, she was not denying her essential equality with him. Peter refers to this incident, yet also says husbands and wives are, "heirs together of the grace of life" (1Pet 3:6f).

Or, a person's "God" is whatever is most important to him (Phil 3:18f; cp. John 4:34). Or, Jesus referred to the Father in this manner due to His human nature and the "kenosis" (Phil 2:6-8).

Also, in Hebrews 1:8, the Father calls the Son "God" (see also Ps 45:6f). And note how Jesus always separates His Sonship from everyone else's ("MY Father and YOUR Father" - "MY God and YOUR God").

1Corinthians 11:3:
"the head of Christ is God" - so the Father is superior to Christ.

BUT: The verse also says, "the head of woman is man." If this verse is teaching the Father is essential superior to Christ, then men are superior to women (but see Gen 1:26f). "Headship" in this verse refers to positional distinctions, not essential relationships.

1Corinthians 15:28:
The Son is subject to, and thus inferior to, the Father.

BUT: In Luke 2:51, Jesus is said to have been "subject" to His earthly parents, but in no way can Jesus be said to have been inferior to Joseph and Mary. In the same way, being subject to His heavenly Father does not mean Jesus is inferior to the Father. Positional, not essential, relationships are being discussed in these verses (see also Eph 6:1-3; Col 3:20).

Colossians 1:15:
The "first-born" is part of the group of which he is the firstborn; so Jesus must be human, not God.

BUT: Christian doctrine says Jesus is fully God AND fully human (two natures in one Person; Col 2:9). So, as a result of the incarnation, Jesus IS "part of the group" of humanity (Heb 2:14-18). But He is still also God (John 1:1,14).

Colossians 1:16,17,20:
The word "all" (Greek, *pas*) should be translated "all other" since it is translated as such in Luke 13:2; 21:29; Phil 2:21. So Paul is not teaching Jesus is distinct from the creation.

BUT: It is questionable if *pas* should be translated as "all other" rather than just "all" in Luke 13:2; 21:29; Phil 2:21. The NKJV only includes "other" in the first of these (and then in italics); the KJV, MKJV, LITV, and ALT do not use "other" in any of these verses. As such, these verses provide precarious proof for translating *pas* as "all other" rather than simply "all" in the three Colossians verses.

Furthermore, *pas* is used hundreds of times elsewhere in the NT and it is almost always translated as simply "all" or "every" -- including the other 33 times it is used in Colossians. See most notably Col 1:15,18,19.

Revelation 3:14:
"the beginning of the creation of God" means Jesus is the first created thing.

BUT: "beginning" is used three other times in the Revelation, and each time it is used in a title referring to God and Him being the "Source" or "Ruler" of the creation (1:8; 21:6; 22:13).

Arguments Against the Spirit's Personality

Matthew 3:11:
Water is impersonal, so the Holy Spirit must be also. And the Spirit is used to baptize. Thus the Spirit cannot be a Person.

BUT: Water is just a symbol. And to be "baptized by the Spirit" means to be "led" by Him (Rom 8:14). And believers are "baptized into Christ Jesus" -- a Person (Rom 6:3).

Romans 8:16:
"He" is literally "it" in the Greek (*autou*). So the Spirit is impersonal.

BUT: The neuter "it" is used because "Spirit" in Greek is neuter (*pneuma*). And in Greek a pronoun must agree with its antecedent in gender and number. So it is just a matter of Greek grammar not theology.

Also, despite "Spirit" being neuter, a masculine pronoun is used in reference to Him in John 14:16; 15:26; 16:8,13f ("He" Greek: *ekeinos*, literal "that One").

Acts 2:17:
The Spirit is "poured out" which a person cannot be.

BUT: David, speaking prophetically of the Messiah, said, "I am poured out ..." (Ps 22:14). And Paul, on two occasions, said he was "being poured out" (Phil 2:17; 2Tim 4:6). So a person can be "poured out."

Acts 2:32:
A person cannot "fill" a person let alone 120 at the same time.

BUT: To be "filled with the Holy Spirit" is to be controlled by Him (Eph 5:18). And since the Spirit is omnipresent (Ps 139:7), He can control as many "as He wills" (1Cor 12:11).

Acts 10:38:
The Spirit is used to "anoint" people, so He cannot be a Person.

BUT: "To anoint," means to appoint someone and set him aside for the service of God. And God regularly uses a person to anoint another person (1Sam 16:3,13). So why can't the first Person of the Trinity (the Father) use the third Person of the Trinity (the Spirit) to "anoint" the second Person of the Trinity (the Son)?

Arguments Against God's "Three-ness"

Deuteronomy 6:4:
God is "one" not three.

BUT: The Trinity doctrine includes God's "oneness." He is one in essence, three in Person. Also, "one" is often used in Scripture for a composite unity (Gen 2:24; Exod 24:3; 26:11; Numb 13:23; Judg 6:16; Rom 12:4f).

Isaiah 9:6:
The Messiah is called "Everlasting Father." Thus the Son and the Father are not distinct Persons.

BUT: The passage is more literally translated as "Father of Eternity" since the word "Father" is before "Eternity" in the Hebrew text. Compare the next phrase, "Prince of Peace" where the same construction occurs. This translation indicates the Son is the origin of time (John 1:3).

Or, "Father" refers to the Messiah's relationship to "us" and our salvation ("For unto US a Child is born").

He is called our "Father" since He is the Author (or Originator) of our salvation (Heb 12:2). His "fatherhood" is "everlasting" since, "He always lives" (Heb 7:25). All who are saved are thus the Messiah's "children" (Ps 22:30; Isa 8:18; 22:21f; 53:10; Heb 2:10-18).

On the other hand, the Messiah is "Son" in His relationship to the Father ("For unto us a SON is given" - cp. John 3:16; Heb 1:2).

Isaiah 43:10:
There is no God besides the Lord, so there cannot be three Gods.

BUT: The Trinity states there is only one God! (three Persons; one God).

John 10:30:
"I and the Father are one" indicates they are the same Person.

BUT: "One" (*ev*) is neuter, not masculine; thus, it cannot indicate oneness of Person.

John 14:9:
Seeing Jesus is the same as seeing the Father since they are the same Person.

BUT: It is the same since they are of the same essence (Heb 1:1-3).

Galatians 1:8:
The teaching of the Trinity is "another gospel" since Paul never preached about the Trinity.

BUT: Paul had much to say regarding the doctrine of the Trinity. See Scripture Study #3 for references from his epistles.

Moreover, in Galatians Paul is discussing the Gospel of salvation by grace alone versus the "gospel" the false teachers promoted of salvation by works (or grace plus works). The subject of the nature and attributes of God is not addressed in the epistle.

Hebrews 1:2:
God is expressed in only one Person, Jesus.

BUT: Verse 1 says God spoke "by the prophets." Verse 2 then says God now has spoken "by His Son." The word "by" (Gr. *en*) is the same in each phrase and indicates instrumentality (*PC Study Bible*). So just as the Father spoke through the prophets but is not the same Person as the prophets, He speaks through His Son but is not the same Person as the Son.

Hebrews 1:3:
Jesus is "the express image" of the Person of God. So God is only one Person, Jesus.

BUT: "express image" (Gr. *charakter*) can mean, "the exact expression (the image) of any person or thing, marked likeness, precise reproduction in every respect" (*Online Bible*). So the verse is teaching Jesus has the same nature and attributes as the Father, not that He is the same Person as the Father.

1John 5:7:
The Father, the Word, and the Holy Spirit are "one" not three Persons.

BUT: The textual difficulty of this verse makes it a precarious proof-text. Nevertheless, even if the verse is genuine "one" (Gr. *ev*) cannot be referring to one Person as the word is neuter, not masculine. As such, it refers to one in essence or one in agreement (see v.8).

1John 5:20:
Jesus is "the true God" not just the Son of God.

BUT: The doctrine of the Trinity states that Jesus is the true God! More specifically, the Father, Son, and Holy Spirit are the three Persons in the one Godhead: three Persons, one true God.

Notes:

Mormons argue against the Trinity by teaching there is more than one God. They believe the Father, Son, and Spirit are three distinct Gods.

Jehovah's Witnesses argue against the Trinity by denying Jesus' Deity and the Spirit's personality. They teach Jesus is a created being ("a god") and the Spirit is just "God's active force."

United Pentecostals and other "Jesus only" groups argue against the Trinity by denying God's "three-ness." They say Father, Son, and Spirit are simply three different modes in which Jesus operates.

Each of these three views is represented in the opposing arguments presented in this study. The sources for the opposing arguments are various publications by the above and other organizations that promote the idea, along with personal conversations and correspondences this writer has had with adherents to the view.

Bibliography:

KJV/ NKJV Parallel Reference Bible. Nashville: Thomas Nelson, 1991.

Jamieson, Fausset and Brown. *Commentary on the Whole Bible.* Grand Rapids, MI: Regency, 1961.

Online Bible. Publ. By Larry Pierce. Winterborne, Ontario, 1996.

PC Study Bible. Seattle, WA: Biblesoft, 1996.

Rienecker. Fritz and Cleon Rogers. *Linguistic Key to the Greek NT*. Grand Rapids, MI: Zondervan, 1980.

Thayer, Joseph. *The New Thayer's Greek-English Lexicon of the NT*. Peabody, MA: Hendrickson Publishers, 1981.

All Scripture references from: *New King James Version*. Nashville, TN: Thomas Nelson Publishers, 1982, unless otherwise indicated.

More on the Trinity

Scripture Study #5

Possible Hints of the Plurality of God in the OT

1) Genesis 1:1 - "God" is a plural noun, but "created" is a singular verb.

2) The Sprit of God in creation:

Gen 1:2: The Spirit "was hovering" over the Creation (cp. Deut 32:11, the only other place in Scripture where the same verb is used).
Job 33:4: The Spirit "makes" people, yet in Gen 2:7, the Lord "formed" human beings.

3) God refers to Himself with first person, plural pronouns: Gen 1:26; 3:22; 11:7; Isa 6:8.

4) Verses indicating there are TWO Lords (Jehovahs):

Gen 19:24; Isa 48:16; Zech 2:6-3:2.

5) Passage indicating there are TWO Gods:

Ps 45:6f (cp. Heb 1:8f). But there is only ONE Lord, and ONE true God (Isa 43:10; 45:5f).

6) Plural verbs (in the Hebrew) are used in reference to God's actions:

Gen 20:13; 35:7.

7) References to the "face" or "presence" of God are actually plural ("faces of God"). The corresponding verbs are also plural in the Hebrew:

Exod 33:14f; Deut 4:37; Ps 27:8f; 31:16,20.

8) "Maker" or "Creator" is plural in the Hebrew in the following verses:

Job 35:10; Ps 149:2; Eccl 12:1; Isa 54:5. But there is only one God and He creates "all alone" (Isa 43:10; 44:24).

9) Use of "the Lord" three and only three times:

Numb 6:24-26; Dan 9:19; Isa 33:22.

10) Three-fold "Holy" used to praise the Lord:

Isa 6:3: Compare Rev 4:8.

11) "Commander of the army of the Lord" -- Josh 5:13-6:2:

Verse 5:14: This heavenly figure is "Commander of the army of the Lord," so He cannot be the same Person as the Lord, yet:
Verse 5:14: Joshua "worshiped" Him.
Verse 5:15: He instructs Joshua to remove his sandals, just as the Lord did to Moses (see Exod 3:5f).
Verse 6:2: The same Person is still speaking and is called "the Lord."

12) Indications of the Messiah's Deity:

Isa 7:14: The Messiah is "God with us."
Isa 9:6: The Messiah is called "Mighty God" -- a phrase used in reference to the Lord in Isa 10:21; Jer 32:17f.

Isa 48:12f,16: The Speaker claims to be the "First and the Last" and to be the Creator, yet the Speaker also says He is sent by the Lord.
Jer 23:5f: The Messiah is "the Lord our Righteousness."
Mic 5:2: The Messiah's "goings forth" are from "everlasting" (Note: "goings forth" does not mean "created" -- the same phrase is used in reference to the Lord in Hos 6:3).
Zech 12:1,10: "The Lord" is speaking and says, "they will look on Me whom they pierced" (cp. Ps 22:16).

13) God has a Son!

Ps 2:7; Prov 30:4: Cp. John 5:18; 19:7 where Jesus is charged with blasphemy for claiming to be "the Son of God."

14) The Word of God in creation:

Ps 33:6: Compare John 1:1-3 where God is said to have made all things "through" the Word, yet God says He created "all alone" (Isa 44:24).

15) The Angel of the Lord and the Lord:

Distinct persons:
2Sam 24:16f; 1Chr 21:15f,27; Zech 1:12.

Same Person:
Gen 22:1f,11f,15f; 28:10-22; 31:11-13; 48:15f (Note: "bless" is singular).
Exod 3:2,4/ Exod 13:21; 14:19.
Exod 20:1; Deut 1:6-8; Judg 2:1.
Judg 6:12-15/ Judg 13:21f.

16) The Holy Spirit and God:

The Spirit and God are distinct:
Neh 9:20; Isa 48:16; Isa 63:11:

47

The Spirit and God are equated:
Exod 29:45f; Hag 2:5:

17) Isaiah 63:7-10:

The Lord is Israel's "Savior" (vv.7,8). But "the Angel of His Presence saved them" (v.9). Meanwhile, the Holy Spirit is "grieved" (v.10).

18) The *Shema*:

Deut 6:4: Even the *Shema* allows for a plurality in the Godhead; "one" can refer to a composite unity: Gen 2:24; Exod 24:3; 26:11; 36:13; Numb 13:21; Judg 6:16 (Note: *shema* is the imperative form of the Hebrew word for "hear").

Note:
The position of the study above is not that the doctrine of the Trinity is fully taught in the OT. But the purpose is to show that the concept of a three-in-one God as taught in the NT is not incompatible with OT monotheism. Or, as *The Believer's Study Bible* states about Isaiah 63:7-10, "... a hint of the triune nature of God more fully presented in the NT" (p.1000).

The Importance of the Trinity

1) The universe:
The unity-diversity in creation reflects the unity-diversity of the Godhead (Note: This is known in philosophical circles as "the one and many problem"):

Gen 1:20-25; Ps 19:1; Rom 1:19f; 1Cor 15:39-41.

2) Human Institutions:

The government of the United States is set up with a separation of powers between three branches. Each of these three branches has a different function or role to perform (cp. Deut 1:9-18; 17:8-11).

This form of government has proven to be stable since it reflects the nature of God. Within the one Godhead there are three distinct Persons. Each Person has a different function or role to perform, especially in regards to our salvation:

Gal 4:4-6; Eph 1:1-7,13f.

3) Love:

We need relational love because we are created in the image of God who is eternal, relational love:

Gen 1:26f; 2:18-24; John 15:9,12; 17:24; Rom 5:5; 1John 4:7-11.

4) Submission:

All human beings are equal in essence; yet, we are commanded to submit to one another. This submission can be done without denying our essential oneness. We know this is possible since the Son submitted to the Father; yet, He is equal to the Father in essence:

Gal 3:28; John 10:30; 4:34; 16:14; Luke 7:8; Rom 13:1-5; Eph 5:21; 6:1-9; Col 3:20-22; Heb 13:7; 1Pet 5:1-5.

5) Need to be humble:

Despite our equality, we are to humble ourselves before one another just as the Son humbled Himself before His equal, God the Father:

Phil 2:3-11.

6) Marriage:

The "oneness" between a husband and wife reflects the oneness between the Father and the Son. It is for this reason that the bond of marriage should not be broken:

Gen 2:24; Duet 6:4; Matt 19:3-6.

The headship of the husband over the wife parallels the headship of the Father over the Son:

1Cor 11:3.

The wife should submit to her husband just as the Son submitted to the will of the Father:

Luke 22:42; Eph 5:22-24; Col 3:18f; 1Pet 3:1-7.

The husband should love his wife as the Father loves the Son and the Son loves the Church:

John 3:35; 5:20; Eph 5:25.

7) The Atonement:

Jesus had to be fully human to stand in our place and receive God the Father's wrath against our sins; He had to be fully God for His sacrifice to be sufficient to pay for all of the sins of all of the children of God:

Isa 53:4-6; John 1:19; 3:36; 11:49-52; Heb 9:24-28; 10:10-14.

8) Mediator:

Due to His full humanity and full Deity and the atonement He has provided, Jesus can mediate before God the Father for us:

Job 9:32f; 1Tim 2:5; Rom 8:34; Heb 2:16-18; 4:14-16; 7:24-28; 9:13-15; 10:19-23; 1John 2:1f.

9) Salvation:

All three Persons of the Godhead are involved in securing our salvation:

Gal 4:4-6; Eph 1:3-4; Titus 3:4-7; Heb 9:14; 1Pet 1:1-5.

10) Relationship with the Triune God:

The Bible teaches it is possible to have a relationship with the Father, the Son, and the Holy Spirit. For this to be possible, each must be omnipresent and omniscience. These two attributes only a Person who is God can possess:

Matt 28:19f; John 17:3; Acts 9:31; Rom 8:9-11,14-16,26f,31-39; 15:30; 2Cor 13:5,14; Heb 13:5f; 1John 1:3; 4:12-16; 5:10-13; Jude 20f.

The Full Humanity of Jesus

1) The Incarnation:

Gen 3:15; Isa 7:14; Matt 1:16,18-25; Luke 1:26-31; John 1:14; Rom 1:3; Gal 4:4; Heb 2:6f,9,17; 10:5.

2) After the Incarnation:

Matt 4:1; 26:38; Mark 13:32; Luke 2:46; John 4:6; 8:40; 11:33-35; 12:27; 19:28-34; Rom 8:3; Phil 2:3-8; Heb 4:15; 1John 1:1-3; 4:1-3; 2John 7.

3) After the Resurrection:

John 2:19-21; 20:19-27; Luke 24:39; Acts 2:22-31; 17:31; Col 2:9; 1Tim 2:5; Rev 1:18.

Bibliography:

All Scripture references from: *The New King James Version*. Nashville, TN: Thomas Nelson Publishers, 1982, unless otherwise indicated.

Criswell, W.A. ed. *The Believer's Study Bible: NKJV.* Nashville, Thomas Nelson, 1991.

More on the Trinity: Scripture Study. Contained in the book *Scripture Workbook*. Copyright © 1999-2000 by Gary F. Zeolla of Darkness to Light ministry - http://www.dtl.org

The Person and Work of Jesus Christ

Scripture Study #6

The Virgin Birth of Jesus Christ

1) Biblical Evidence for the Virgin Birth:

Genesis 3:15:

Here is the first promise of a coming Redeemer. God promises the Seed of the WOMAN will defeat the serpent (Satan). This is the only passage in the OT where there is a reference to the "seed" of a woman. Elsewhere, it is always worded as referring to the seed of a man (see Gen 21:12f; 22:18; 26:4; 28:14; Dan 2:43).

Isaiah 7:14:

The word rendered "virgin" in this verse does not refer to simply a "young woman" as some claim. In all other usages of the word in the OT, the preferred meaning is "virgin" - see Gen 24:43 (cp. v.16); Exod 2:8; Ps 68:25; Prov 30:19; Song 1:3; 6:8.

Also, the Lord is declaring He is giving a "sign" to Israel. There is no sign in a woman conceiving in the normal manner. But for a virgin to conceive...

And finally, when Matthew quotes this verse, he uses the Greek word for "virgin" in translating the original Hebrew word (Matt 1:23).

Matthew 1:16:

Joseph is not said to have "begot" Jesus. He is simply called "the husband of Mary" since Joseph is Jesus' stepfather, not His biological father.

Moreover, the phrase, "of whom" is a FEMININE word in the Greek. If Joseph were involved in the conception of Jesus, correct Greek grammar would have demanded a masculine pronoun.

Matthew 1:18-25:

Mary becomes pregnant before she and Joseph "came together" (an euphemism for sexual intercourse). Moreover, twice in this passage, Mary's conception is said to be "of the Holy Spirit" (vv.18,20).

Luke 1:26-38:

Mary is specifically called a "virgin" (v.27). She is to conceive Jesus even though she has never "known a man" (again, an euphemism for sexual intercourse). The angel tells her she will conceive because, "The Holy Spirit will come upon you" (v.35). This is similar to Matthew's statement that Jesus was conceived, "of the Holy Spirit."

John 8:41:

The Pharisees are hinting to Jesus that His birth was illegitimate. Since less than nine months passed between the time Mary and Joseph were married and when Jesus was born (Luke 1:56; 2:4-6), there were probably rumors floating around as to how He was conceived.

2) The Importance of the Virgin Birth:

The Virgin Birth enabled Jesus to be both God AND man. The importance of this dual nature to the one Person of Christ is outline in Scripture Study #5.

3) The Full Humanity of Jesus Christ:

Matt 4:1; 26:38; Mark 13:32; Luke 2:46; John 1:14; 4:6; 8:40; 11:33-35; 12:27; 19:28-34; Rom 1:3; 8:3; Phil 2:3-8; Heb 2:6f,9,17; 4:15; 10:5; 1John 1:1-3; 4:1-3; 2John 7.

The Resurrection of Jesus Christ

1) Was Jesus Raised with a Physical or an Immaterial Body?

An Immaterial Body (Jehovah's Witnesses, some New Age groups):

1Corinthians 15:44:
    Paul teaches human beings in general, which would include Jesus, are raised with "spiritual" bodies.

BUT: "Spiritual" does not necessarily mean "immaterial" but simply newness. So Paul is saying our resurrected bodies will be similar to, but not identical with, our present bodies (see verses 39-43).

1Corinthians 15:50:
    "flesh and blood cannot inherit the kingdom of God" so Jesus could not have been resurrected bodily.

BUT: "flesh and blood" was simply an idiom for our present, frail, mortal existence. The idiom of the time used to refer to a physical body was "flesh and bones" (see discussion on Luke 24:39 below; Blomberg, p.109).

Acts 10:40,41:

Only a select few saw the resurrected Jesus. And they were able to see Him only because He "materialized" a physical body while in their presence.

BUT: There is an easier explanation for why others did not see Jesus; He simply did not come within their sight! And remember, over 500 people DID see Him (1Cor 15:6).

Hebrews 10:10:

Jesus offered His body "once for all" so He cannot still have it.

BUT: The point of the "once for all" in this verse is to indicate Jesus does not have to die again for our sins (see vv. 11-14). The nature of the resurrection is not even being discussed.

1Peter 3:18:

Christ was "made alive in the spirit" not in a physical body.

BUT: The phrase can also be translated, "by the Spirit" (KJV, NKJV), or "in the Spirit" (MKJV, LITV). With either of these renderings, the passage is simply teaching God the Holy Spirit was involved in resurrecting Christ.

The contrast would then be that Christ truly died a physical death, but He rose by (or, in) the power of the Spirit.

Luke 24:13-32; John 20:11-18; 21:1-14:

In His post-resurrection appearances, Jesus was not immediately recognized since He was appearing in different bodies.

BUT: A careful reading of each passage will show the problem was not due to Jesus appearing in different bodies but was elsewhere:

Luke 24:13-32:

On the road to Emmaus, the reason the disciples did not recognize Jesus was because, "their eyes were restrained, so that they did not know Him" (v.16). They "knew Him" when, "their eyes were opened" (v.31; cp. Gen 21:19).

John 20:11-18:

In the case of Mary Magdalene, it says twice in the passage she was weeping (vv. 13,15). When Jesus spoke her name, she had to turn around in order to be facing Him (v.16). A woman with tear-filled eyes is not very likely to recognize someone she isn't even looking at! And remember, she expected to find Jesus in a horizontal, not vertical position (Mark 16:1).

John 21:1-14:

As for the episode at the Sea of Tiberias, the disciples are in a boat in the middle of the lake while Jesus is standing on the shore (vv.3,4). Also, it was daybreak (v.4). This would mean the light was still dim and possibly haze was rising from the lake.

Further, the disciples were exhausted and frustrated from working all night to no avail (v.3). With these conditions, it is easy to understand why the disciples had difficulty recognizing Jesus.

A Physical Body:

Luke 24:33-43:

When Jesus appeared to the disciples they were frightened because they thought they were seeing a spirit (v.37). Jesus calmed them by declaring, "Behold my hands and my feet, that it is I myself. Handle me and see, for a spirit does not have flesh and bones as you see that I have" (v.39). Be sure to note the phrase, "flesh and bones" and compare the discussion on 1Cor 15:50 above.

John 2:18-22:

At the beginning of His ministry, Jesus predicted, "Destroy this temple and in three days I will raise it up." John then explains, "He was speaking of the temple of HIS BODY."

John 20:26-29:

Upon appearing to "doubting" Thomas, Jesus challenged him to, "Reach your finger here, and look at My hands; and reach your hand here, and put it into My side. Do not unbelieving, but believing." Thomas' reaction was to say to Jesus, "My Lord and my God!"

Acts 2:22-32:

Peter preaches about Jesus, "His soul was not left in Hades, nor did His flesh see corruption" (v.31). This contrasts with David's remains (v.29).

Acts 17:31; 1Tim 2:5:

Paul calls Jesus a "Man" years after the resurrection.

Colossians 2:9:

"For in Him DWELLS all the fullness of the Godhead BODILY." This was written about 30 years after the resurrection, but note the present tense "dwells."

2) The Purposes of the Resurrection of Jesus Christ:

Matthew 12:38-42:
Christ's resurrection would be the "sign" upholding the truthfulness of His preaching ministry, and it would show the Jews their need to repent for rejecting Him.

John 2:13-22:
Christ's resurrection would be the "sign" His actions were appropriate (vv.18-21).

Acts 2:22-36:
Christ's resurrection showed He was the fulfillment of the OT prophecies about the Messiah (vv.25-32). Further, it showed Jesus had been exalted to the right hand of God (v.33). As a result, He is "both Christ and Lord" (v.36).

Acts 17:30,31:
Christ's resurrection shows there is a need for "all men everywhere to repent" since there is "a day on which (God) will judge the world in righteousness."

Romans 1:3,4:
Christ's resurrection demonstrated He is "the Son of God."

Romans 4:22-25:
Christ's resurrection is proof we can be imputed righteousness, receive forgiveness for our offenses, attain justification, and have peace with God simply "by faith" (5:1).

Romans 5:10:
Christ's resurrection shows we can be "reconciled to God."

1Corinthians 15:20-23:
Christ's resurrection demonstrates there is coming a "resurrection of the dead."

The Second Coming of Jesus Christ

1) What Will Be the Nature of Jesus' Return?

Spiritual, Immaterial, and Invisible (Jehovah's Witnesses, some New Age groups):

Matthew 24:3:
"Coming" can also be translated "presence." So Jesus is only talking about the time when His presence or influence will be felt on the earth.

BUT: What does "presence" mean? The same Greek word is used in the following passages and refers to a bodily "coming" of a person to others resulting in his "presence" among them: 1Cor 16:17; 2Cor 7:6f; 10:10; Phil 1:26; 2:12. And the word is even used in reference to Jesus' FIRST "coming"--which was in a body! (2Pet 1:16).

John 14:19:
Jesus says, "the world" will never see Him again.

BUT: In Acts 20:37 the Ephesian elders were sorrowful because they knew they would not see Paul again. Yet, in heaven or at the resurrection all believers will see one another again. So Paul's and Jesus' words only refer to this current age, not the age to come.

Personal, Physical, and Visible:

Zechariah 12:10:
The Messiah is speaking and says about the Jewish race, "they will LOOK ON ME whom they have pierced."

Matthew 24:23-27:
When people say, "Look, here is the Christ" they are not to be believed since the Second Coming will be a visible event no one will miss.

Matthew 24:30:
People "will SEE the Son of Man coming...."

Acts 1:9-11:
Jesus ascended in a physical and bodily manner and will return, "in like manner."

1Corinthians 4:5:
Paul says Christ is going to "come" in judgment. He uses the same word about himself later in the same chapter to refer to his planned, second visit to the Corinthians (vv. 18-21).

2Timothy 4:1,8; Titus 2:13:
Paul refers to Jesus' return as an "appearing."

Hebrews 9:28:
Christ "will appear a second time."

Revelation 1:7:
Christ "is coming" and "every eye will see Him."

2) No One Knows the Time of the Second Coming:

Deut 29:29; Matt 24:36,42-44; 25:1-13; Mark 13:32-37; Acts 1:7; 1Thes 5:2; 2Pet 3:10.

Bibliography:
All Scripture references from: *The New King James Version*. Nashville, TN: Thomas Nelson Publishers, 1982, unless otherwise indicated.

Blomberg, Craig. The Historical Reliability of the Gospels. Downer's Grove, IL: InterVarsity Press, 1987.

Person and Life of Jesus Christ: Scripture Study. Contained in the book *Scripture Workbook*. Copyright © 1999-2000 by Gary F. Zeolla of Darkness to Light ministry - http://www.dtl.org

Sin, Atonement, and Salvation

Scripture Study #7

Sin

1) **Sin:** "Any act, attitude, or disposition which fails to completely fulfill or measure up to the standards of God's righteousness. It may involve an actual transgression of God's law or failure to live up to His norms" (Erickson, p.152).

In the OT: Exod 20:1-21; Lev 5:17; 6:1-7; 18:1-30; 26:14-46; Numb 32:23; Deut 28:15-68; Ps 38:3-8; 51:4; 90:7-12; Isa 59:2; Jer 2:22; 3:12,3; 5:21-29; Ezek 18:4.

In the NT: Matt 5:17-48; 6:24; 7:21-23; Luke 6:46; 12:2,3; Rom 1:18-32; 6:23; 1Cor 6:9,10; Gal 3:10; 5:19-21; Col 3:5-9; Jam 1:26,27; 4:1-4,17; 1John 1:5,6; 3:4.

2) **Original sin:** "... a hereditary depravity and corruption of our nature, diffused into all parts of the soul, which first makes us liable to God's wrath, then also brings forth in us those works which Scripture calls 'works of the flesh'" (Gal 5:19; Calvin, p.251).

In the OT: Gen 3:1-20; 6:5; 8:21; Ps 51:5; 58:3; Jer 16:12; 17:9; Eccl 9:3.

In the NT: Matt 15:19,20; John 3:36; Rom 5:12-21; Eph 2:3; Jam 1:13-15.

3) **Every person has sinned:**

In the OT: 1Ki 8:46; Ps 53:2,3; 130:3,4; 143:2; Pr 20:9; Eccl 7:20; Isa 53:6; 64:6.

In the NT: Rom 3:10-18,23; Gal 3:22; Jam 3:2; 1John 1:8-10.

4) Other Aspects of Sin:

Breaking our promises is sin: Numb 30:2; Deut 23:21-23; Acts 5:1-11.
Breaking our own standards is sin: Matt 7:2; Rom 2:1-3,12-16; 14:23; Jam 2:13.
Unbelief is sin: John 3:17-21; Heb 3:12,16-19; 12:1; Rev 21:8.
Sin enslaves: Prov 5:21-23; John 8:34; Acts 8:23; Rom 6:16-18; 2Pet 2:18,19.

5) Repentance: "Repentance is that change of a sinner's mind which leads him to turn from his evil ways and live.... Man must apprehend sin as unutterably heinous, the Divine law as perfect and inexorable [unchangeable], and himself as coming short or falling below the requirements of a holy God" (Byron DeMent, in Green, p.953).

In the OT: Deut 30:1-3; 1Sam 7:3; Job 42:1-6; Ps 38:17,18; 41:4; 51:1-17; Isa 55:7; Jer 25:5; Ezek 14:6; 18:30-32; 33:11; Jonah 3:4-10.

In the NT: Matt 3:8; 9:13; 21:28-32; Mark 1:14,15; 6:12; Luke 3:7-9; 5:32; 13:1-5; 18:9-14; 24:46,47; Acts 3:19; 8:22; 11:18; 17:30; 20:21; 26:19,20; Rom 2:4; 6:13; 13:12-14; 2Cor 7:9-11; 1Thes 1:9; Heb 6:1; Rev 2:5,16,21-23; 3:19; 9:20,21; 16:9-11.

Atonement

1) Atonement: "Atonement is the term which has come to be widely used to denote the substitutionary work of Christ which culminated in the sacrifice of Calvary."

Pre-figured in the OT: Gen 3:14,15,21; 4:4,5; 22:6-14; Exod 12:21-23; 29:38,39; Lev 1:3-5; 4:1-7; 5:5-9; 16:11-17; 17:11; Ps 22:14-18; Isa 53:4-12; Zech 12:10.
Fulfilled in the NT: Matt 27:35,45-54; John 19:30; 1Cor 15:1-8; Heb 7:25-27; 10:11-14; 1Pet 2:24; Rev 5:8-14.

2) Different Aspects of the Atonement: "... no one term can express the manifold aspects from which, according to Scripture, this work of Christ must be viewed."

Obedience: Christ's obedience qualified Him to be the sacrifice for sin: Ps 40:6-8; Matt 26:38-44; John 4:34; 6:38; Rom 5:19; 2Cor 5:21; Phil 2:5-8; Heb 5:7-10; 10:5-10.

Sacrifice: Christ's giving of Himself was a sacrificial offering for sin: Isa 52:13-53:12; John 1:29; 1Cor 5:7; Eph 5:2; Heb 7:26-28; 9:14,24-28; 10:11-14.

Ransom: Christ paid the ransom price to free His people from sin: Matt 1:21; 20:28; Mark 10:45; John 11:49-52; 1Tim 2:5,6.

Redemption: "Redemption has in view the bondage to which sin has consigned us."
Redemption from the curse of sin: Rom 3:24; 4:25; 8:23; 1Cor 1:30; Gal 3:13,14; 4:5; Eph 1:3-14; 4:30; Col 1:13,14; Heb 9:12-15; 1Pet 1:18,19; Rev 5:9,10.

Redemption from the power of sin: Rom 6:1-14; 13:11-14; 1Cor 6:20; 2Cor 5:14-17; Eph 2:10; Titus 2:11-14; 1Pet 1:13-25; 1John 3:1-9.

Propitiation: "To propitiate means to pacify, to conciliate, to make propitious.... God so loved the objects of His wrath that He gave His own Son to the end that He by His blood should make provision for the removal of this wrath."
John 3:16-18,36; Rom 3:25; 5:8,9; Eph 2:1-7; Heb 2:17; 1John 2:2; 4:10.

Forgiveness: Sins can be forgiven as a result of the work of Christ on the cross: Matt 26:28; Acts 10:43; 13:38; 26:18; Eph 1:7; Col 2:13,14; Heb 9:22; 1John 1:9.

Reconciliation: "... reconciliation is concerned with our alienation from God and the need of having that alienation removed." Rom 5:1,10; 2Cor 5:18-21; Eph 2:14-18; Col 1:21,22; Heb 4:14-16 (quotes in above section from John Murray, in Green, pp.146-154).

Salvation

"... to be saved as Christ saves, is to have all our innumerable sins and transgressions forgiven and blotted out; all those heavy loads of guilt which oppressed our souls perfectly removed from our minds. It is to be reconciled to God.... It is to have a new principle of life infused into our souls" (Green, pp.978,9).

1) Salvation is by grace through faith:

Mark 10:26,27; Luke 1:76-79; John 1:12; 3:14-18,36, 5:24; 6:28,29; 20:30,31; Acts 15:8-11; 16:30,31; Rom 1:16,17; 3:27-4:8; 11:6; Gal 2:16; 3:1-11,26; Eph 2:4-10; 2Tim 1:8,9; Titus 3:3-7; Heb 4:8-10; 11:5,6.

2) Salvation is only through Jesus Christ:

Matt 7:13,14,21-23; 11:27; 28:18-20; Mark 16:15,16; Luke 24:46,47; John 3:13-18,36; 5:22,23; 10:9; 14:6; 15:23; 20:30,31; Acts 4:12; 10:43; 17:30; Eph 2:11-13; 1Tim 2:5; 1John 2:23; 5:11,12.

3) Born-again/ regeneration:

Ezek 36:25-27; John 1:12,13; 3:3-8; Rom 8:6-11,16,17; 12:2; 1Cor 6:11,19,20; 2Cor 5:l7; Eph 4:17-24; Titus 3:5; 1Pet 1:22,23; 1John 3:1-3; 5:1.

4) Assurance of salvation:

Job 19:25,26; Ps 23:4; John 10:27-29; Rom 7:24-8:39; 1Cor 10:13; 2Cor 4:16-5:8; Heb 4:14-16; 10:19-23; 1John 5:12,13; Jude 24,25.

"HOW SHALL WE ESCAPE IF WE NEGLECT
SO GREAT A SALVATION ...?"
(Hebrews 2:3)

Bibliography:
All Scripture references from: *The New King James Version*. Nashville, TN: Thomas Nelson Publishers, 1982, unless otherwise indicated.

Calvin, John. *Institutes of the Christian Religion*. Vol.I. Philadelphia: Westminster, 1960.

Erickson, Millard J. *Concise Dictionary of Christian Theology*. Grand Rapids: Baker Book House: 1986.

Green, J.P. ed. *The Classic Bible Dictionary*. Lafayette, IN: Sovereign Grace Trust Fund, 1988.

The Afterlife

Scripture Study #8

1) Is there conscious existence after death?

No (This view is sometimes referred to as "soul-sleep" -- Jehovah's Witnesses, Seventh-Day Adventists):

Psalm 146:4:
   A person's "thoughts" perish at death.

BUT: The word is better translated "plans" (see Job 17:11; Ps 33:10f; Pr 11:7 where the same word is used). This verse means the "plans" someone had for this life will not be accomplish when he dies.

Ecclesiastes 9:5:
   "the dead know nothing" -- thus they are unconscious.

BUT: If this verse means the dead are unconscious, then 9:6 denies the resurrection of the dead. Up until the last chapter, Ecclesiastes presents what life is like if one views it from a non-biblical perspective.

   Is there really nothing better "than to eat, drink, and be merry?" (8:5; cp. Luke 12:19f). If one has the attitude of the Preacher then, "Vanity of vanities; all is vanity" (1:1f).

Psalm 115:17:
   "The dead do not praise the Lord" since they are unconscious.

BUT: The purpose of this Psalm is not to contrast the living versus the dead. It is designed to contrast the worship of Israel with the worship of "the nations" (v.2). The nations worship dead idols (vv.4-8), but Israel worships the Lord (vv. 9-12).

Verse 17 is saying "the dead" of the nations have lost their chance to come to know and worship the true God. But the people of Israel know the true God and thus can, "bless the Lord from this time forth and forevermore" (v.17).

Yes:

In the OT:

Genesis 25:8:
When Abraham died he, "was gathered to his people" (see also Gen 25:17; 35:29; 49:33).

Deuteronomy 18:10,11:
Israel is forbidden to tolerate those, "who call up the dead."

1Samuel 8:3-20:
After Samuel's death, Saul, in disobedience to God's command, asks a medium to, "Bring up Samuel for me" (v.11). Samuel then appears and speaks to Saul (vv. 12-18).

Note: Whether the dead are actually conjured up in a seance is not the issue. The above two verses show the Jews thought the dead are conscious and thus could be contacted.

2Samuel 12:15-23:
David stops weeping after his son's death since he believes that someday he will "go to" him. Would knowing he was going to join his son in unconsciousness give David such comfort?

Job 26:5; Isaiah 14:9:
"The dead tremble" and can be "stirred up." Would these actions be possible if the dead are unconscious?

In the NT:
Hades is the place of the dead between death and resurrection. It is used in the following verses in the NT:

Matt 11:23; 16:18; Luke 10:15; 16:23; Acts 2:27,31; 1Cor 15:55; Rev 1:18; 6:8; 20:13f.

Other pertinent verses in the NT:

Matthew 17:3:
Were Moses and Elijah raised from unconsciousness just for this event and then immediately afterwards put back to "sleep?"

Luke 16:19-31:
In this passage, Jesus describes Hades as a place of "torments" (v.23). And the rich man in Hades is able to see and converse with others (vv. 23-31). The force of this passage cannot be evaded by saying it is just a parable. First off, in none of His parables does Jesus ever name one of the characters as He does here ("Lazarus" - v.20).

Secondly, the purpose of a parable is to use a situation the hearers know about from first hand experience to describe a spiritual truth. But how many living people have experienced dying and going to Hades? Given these points, Jesus is most likely referring to two men who had recently died and whom His hearers had known.

Luke 23:43:

Jesus is telling the thief on the cross that "TODAY you will be with Me in Paradise." So the thief would have consciousness immediately after death and not only after the resurrection.

This passage cannot be evaded by re-punctuating the verse as "Assuredly, I say to you today," putting the word "today" in the introductory clause rather than the main clause. This rendering would make the 'today" being just Jesus saying when He was talking and not when the thief will be in paradise.

But forty-one other times in the synoptic Gospels Jesus is recorded as prefacing a statement with "Assuredly, I say to you." But in none of those incidences does He add the word "today." So it must be asked, why would Jesus, while hanging on the cross and fighting for every breath, change His pattern and add this unnecessary word about when He was talking? When else would He be talking, tomorrow?

John 8:56:

Abraham must be conscious to be able to "see" Jesus' day.

John 14:2,3; 17:24:

Jesus is going to heaven to "prepare a place" for us so that we will be with Him there.

Romans 14:9:

Christ is "Lord of the dead" which doesn't make much sense if the dead do not exist or are "asleep."

Philippians 1:22-24:
Paul has a "desire to depart and be with Christ" not to "depart" and be unconscious.

2Corinthians 5:6-8:
It is the Christian's desire to be "absent from the body and to be present with the Lord."

1Thessalonians 4:14:
"those who sleep in Jesus" is a reference to the appearance of the physical bodies of Christians who have died, not their souls. And note, these souls will be with Jesus before the resurrection.

1Thessalonians 5:9,10:
Even if we "sleep" in death we are still with Jesus.

Hebrews 12:1,2:
We are surrounded by the "cloud" of OT witnesses.

Hebrews 12:22,23:
When Christians die they meet God and "the spirits of just men made perfect."

1Peter 1:3,4:
Our inheritance is "reserved in heaven" which we could not enjoy much if we are "asleep."

2Peter 2:9:
The unjust are "reserved under punishment" which is rather meaningless if they are not conscious to experience it.

Revelation 6:9-11; 7:9-17:
The dead are "crying out with a loud voice" which is rather impossible if they are "asleep."

2) Related question: Is there a distinction between the spirit/soul and the body?

No (Jehovah's Witnesses, Seventh-Day Adventists):

Genesis 1:20,21:
Literal translation refers to animals as "souls." Hence, the "soul" is simply the life principle shared by animals and people.

BUT: This argument leaves no difference between the human soul and an animal's soul. Yet, there is a clear difference between the two (Gen 2:7,19; 9:5-7; 27:4; Lev 5:17; 20:6; Deut 6:5; 26:16; 30:1-10; Matt 10:31).

Genesis 2:7:
Humans beings were created as "living souls" not as beings with a distinct soul and body.

BUT: Use of synecdoche, a figure of speech where a part is used to designate the whole.

Ezekiel 18:4:
Souls "die" when the body does.

BUT: This passage is referring to spiritual, not physical death (see vv.18:9,13,17,21). Also, the argument assumes "death" means "unconsciousness." But "death" in Scripture refers to "separation." Physical death occurs when the spirit separates from the body (James 2:26).

Spiritual death is a person being separated from his Creator (Gen 2:16f; 3:6-10,24; Ps 73:27f; Matt 27:46; John 11:25f; Luke 15:24; Eph 2:1,5; Col 2:13; Rev 20:6; 21:8; 22:14f).

Yes:

In the OT:

Gen 35:18; Numb 27;16; 2Sam 11:11; 1Kings 17:20-22; Job 4:18f; Ps 32:2; 42:5; Eccl 12:7; Isa 26:9; Dan 7:15; Zech 12:1.

In the NT:

Matt 10:28 (cp. Luke 12:4f); Luke 8:55; 12:46f; 23:46; Acts 7:59; 17:16; 1Cor 2:11; 5:5; 2Cor 4:16; 12:1-4; 1Thes 4:4 (cp. 1Peter 3:7); James 2:26; 2Peter 2:14 (cp. John 21:18f); 3John 2.

Bibliography:
All Scripture references from: *New King James Version*. Nashville, TN: Thomas Nelson Publishers, 1982, unless otherwise indicated.

The Afterlife: Scripture Study. Contained in the book *Scripture Workbook*. Copyright © 1999-2000 by Gary F. Zeolla of Darkness to Light ministry - http://www.dtl.org

Eternity

Scripture Study #9

1) Is there everlasting, conscious torment for the wicked?

No (Jehovah's Witnesses, Seventh-Day Adventists):

Psalm 37:9,22:
> The wicked are "cut-off."

BUT: The reference is to being "cut-off" from life on earth. The eternal state is not in view (compare the use of the same word in Gen 9:11; Isa 11:13; Dan 9:26).

Psalm 104:35:
> The wicked are "consumed."

BUT: Again, the reference is to end of life on earth, not the eternal stare (cp. Num 14:35; Jer 14:15f; 44:12).

Isaiah 47:14; Nahum 1:10:
> The wicked are made "as stubble" and are "devoured."

BUT: These passages refer to the destruction of Babylon and Ninevah respectively, not the eternal state (see Isa 47:1; Nah 1:1).

Obadiah 16:
> The wicked "shall be as though they had never been."

BUT: Again, a reference to the temporal destruction of a wicked city, not the eternal state (see v.1).

Malachi 4:1-3:
The ashes of the wicked are trampled on by the righteous. Thus, the wicked are not conscious.

BUT: This passage refers to events at the Second Coming. It is not describing the eternal state of the wicked after the final judgment.

Matthew 10:28; John 3:16:
The wicked "perish" or are "destroyed."

BUT: The word used in these types of passages does not mean, "pass out of existence" as is assumed by this argument. The same word is translated "lost" elsewhere.

In Matt 10:6, "The LOST sheep of the house of Israel" have not ceased to exist. They are SEPARATED from their God. In Luke 15:4-10, the "lost" objects have been separated from their owners. The prodigal son was separated from his father (Luke 15:24,32). The wicked "perish" or are "destroyed" because they are eternally separated from their God, Owner, and Father (cp. Numb 16:31-35).

Matthew 25:46:
"Punishment" should actually be translated "cutting off."

BUT: The only other use of this noun is in John 4:18. The verbal form of the word occurs twice, in Acts 4:12 and 2Pet 2:9. "Punishment" (or a similar translation) is most appropriate in each of these passages. Also note, the duration of the fate of the wicked is the same as that of the righteous; the same word is used in reference to both.

Romans 6:23:
Death" is the punishment for the wicked, not everlasting torment.

BUT: What is "death?" In Scripture it refers to separation. Physical death is when the spirit separates from the body (James 2:26). Spiritual death is being separated from God (Gen 2:16f; 3:6-10,24; Ps 73:27f; Matt 27:46; John 11:25f; Luke 15:24; Eph 2:1,5; Col 2:13; Rev 20:6; 21:8; 22:14f).

1John 4:8:

"God is love." He could never punish anyone eternally.

BUT: The Bible also says, "Vengeance is Mine, I will repay says the Lord.... It is a fearful thing to fall into the hands of the living God" (Heb 10:30f). Sin against an infinite God demands an infinite punishment. Hence why an infinite sacrifice was needed to atone for sin (Heb 7:25-28). Those not covered by Christ's sacrifice receive the wrath of God (John 3:36). We must accept God's definition of His love and not impose ours onto Him (1John 4:10).

Jude 7:

The fire of Sodom and Gomorrah went out after there was nothing left to burn. In the same way, the fire of torment will go out when the wicked have been annihilated.

BUT: The fire of Sodom and Gomorrah is just "an example." Analogies are not to be forced too far. See also Mark 9:43-48; Rev 14:9-11.

Revelation 14:9-11; 19:3; 20:10:

"Forever" in Scripture can mean only a limited amount of time (Exod 21:6; 1Sam 1:22; Jonah 2:6). So these verses in the Revelation do not teach the torment of the wicked never ends.

BUT: All these references are to a HEBREW WORD in the OT (*olam*). The verses under discussion are in the NT and use a GREEK PHRASE (*tous aionas ton aionon* - "forever and ever"). This phrase is used 11 other times in the Revelation: 10 times in reference to the existence, worship, or reign of Jesus or God (1:6,18; 4:9f; 5:13f; 7:12; 10:6; 11:15; 15:7) and once in reference to the final state of the righteous (22:5).

Revelation 14:10; 20:10:
"Tormented" does not mean experiencing pain but passing into non-existence.

BUT: The word is used three other times in the Revelation and clearly is being used to describe conscious pain (9:5; 11:10; 12:2).

Yes:

1) Gehenna:

Transliteration of the Hebrew for the valley of Hinnom (2Chr 28:3). At the time of Christ it was a place outside of Jerusalem for the disposal of refuse. It burned continually and provided an analogy for the place the wicked are cast into after the final judgment. Gehenna is usually translated "hell."

Gehenna occurs in the following verses in the NT: Matt 5:22,29f; 10:28; 18:9; 23:15,33; Mark 9:43,45,47; Luke 12:5; Jam 3:6.

2) The Lake of Fire:

This phrase is equivalent to Gehenna and occurs in following verses: Rev 19:20; 20:10,14f; 21:8.

3) Phrases used by Jesus to describe existence in hell:

"weeping and gnashing of teeth" Matt 8:12; 13:41f,50; 22:13; 24:51; 25:30; Luke 13:28.

"Their worm does not die and the fire is not quenched"
Mark 9:43-48.

4) Other pertinent passages:

Isa 33:1; Dan 12:2; Matt 25:41,46; John 5:28f; Rom 2:5-10;
Heb 10:29; 2Pet 2:4-9; Jude 6f,13; Rev 14:9-11; 16:8-11;
22:15.

2) Does the Bible teach reincarnation or resurrection?

Note: Reincarnation teaches each person will live many lives, have many deaths, and many judgment (after each death to determine what their state in their next lifetime will be). Resurrection teaches we each have only one life, one death, and one final judgment. Our state throughout eternity will be determined by that one judgment.

Reincarnation (New Age Movement)

Matthew 11:13f:
John the Baptist was Elijah reincarnated.

BUT: The two are equated since John came "in the spirit and power of Elijah" which is a reference to his fiery preaching (Luke 1:17; John 10:41). In Matt 17:3, Elijah is still Elijah (and Moses is still Moses). Also, Elijah did not die, so he could not be reincarnated as John the Baptist (2Kings 2:1,11).

John 9:1f:
The disciples believed in reincarnation; otherwise, this question makes no sense.

BUT: Jesus rebukes them for the question. The question came about do to a prevailing (wrong) belief of many Jews of the time that physical ailments are always due to sin. However, this attitude couldn't account for birth defects (since they didn't believe in reincarnation). Hence the confusion and question of the disciples.

Revelation 3:12:
"Go out no more" implies reincarnation.

BUT: An allusion to the frequent earthquakes in the area. The phrase indicates the ultimate security of "he who overcomes" (cp. 1John 5:4f).

Resurrection:

2Samuel 12:23:
David knows his departed infant son is not coming back to earth again. However, David is confident he will see his son again in the hereafter.

Luke 16:19-31:
There is not even a hint in this passage that the rich man is going to have a "second chance" on earth. His fate in eternity is set. In addition, his hope is that Lazarus will rise from the dead to warn his brothers.

Hebrews 9:27:
One death, one judgment. It couldn't be much clearer!

Daniel 12:2:
"everlasting life" or "everlasting contempt" await us in the future, not an endless round of reincarnations.

John 5:28:
"the resurrection of life" or "the resurrection of condemnation" awaits us in the future.

1Corinthians 15:1-4:
Reincarnation always includes the idea people can pay for their own sins. But if this were possible, Jesus' death would have been unnecessary. But Jesus' death, burial and resurrection comprise "the Gospel."

1Corinthians 15:16-23:
Christ's bodily resurrection from the dead prefigures our resurrection. And each of us will be raised "in his own order" not over and over again.

1Thessalonians 4:13-17:
To comfort the bereaved, Paul assures them that their departed loved ones will be resurrected.

Revelation 20:12-14:
A description of a one-time, end-time resurrection and judgment.

Revelation 20:15; 21:8; 22:15:
Reincarnation usually leads to the idea everyone will ultimately be saved. But the Bible clearly teaches otherwise.

3) Is there going to be a literal "new heavens and new earth?"

No (Jehovah's Witnesses):

Psalm 104:5:
The earth "will not be moved forever."

BUT: Ps 102:25-27 contrasts the eternal, unchanging nature of God with the non-eternal, changeable nature of the universe. So the earth is not eternal and is to undergo a substantial change even if in some way its "foundations" remain the same.

Isaiah 57:20:

"The wicked are like the troubled sea." So in Rev 21:1 where it says, "there was no more sea" it refers to there being no more wicked.

BUT: The Greek words used in Isa 57:20 in the LXX are completely different from those used in Rev 21:1.

Yes:

Genesis 8:22:

God promises, "While the earth remains ... day and night shall not cease." In the new earth, "There shall be no night" (Rev 22:5).

Psalm 102:25-27:

The eternal, unchanging nature of God is contrasted with the non-eternal, changeable nature of the universe.

Isaiah 24:17-23; 51:6; 65:17:

Various references to events at the end of time.

Matthew 5:18:

Heaven and earth will "pass away" when "all is fulfilled."

Matthew 24:35:

"Heaven and earth will pass away"--what more needs to be said?

2Peter 3:10-13:

"the heavens will pass away with a great noise, and the elements will melt with fervent heat" -- sounds rather catastrophic.

Revelation 21:1:

In the new earth there shall be "no more sea." Yet, on this earth, God's "king" will have dominion "from sea to sea" (Ps 72:8; Note: the Greek word for "sea" in the LXX for Ps 72:8 is identical to the word used in Rev 21:1).

Bibliography:

All Scripture references from: *The New King James Version*. Nashville, TN: Thomas Nelson Publishers, 1982, unless otherwise indicated.

Angels, Demons, and the Occult

Scripture Study #10

Angels

1) Every reference to "angel" or "angels" in the Bible:

In the OT:

The Torah: Gen 16:7-11; 19:1,15; 21:17; 22:11-15; 24:7,40; 28:12; 31:11; 32:1; 48:16; Exod 3:2; 14:19, 23:20-23; 32:34; 33:2; Numb 20:16; 22:22-35.

Historical Books: Judges 2:1-4; 5:23; 6:11-22; 13:3-21; 1Sam 29:9; 2Sam 14:17-20; 24:16f; 1Kings 13:18; 19:5-7; 2Kings 1:3,15; 19:35; 1Chron 21:12-30; 32:21.

Poetic Books: Job 4:18; Ps 8:5; 34:7; 35:5f; 78:25,49; 91:11; 103:20; 104:4; 148:2.

Prophetic Books: Isa 37:36; 63:9; Dan 3:28; 6:22; Hos 12:4; Zech 1:9-19; 2:3; 3:1-6; 4:1-5; 5:5,10; 6:4f; 12:8.

In the NT:

The Gospels: Matt 1:20-24; 2:13,19; 4:6,11; 13:39,41,49; 16:27; 18:10; 22:30; 24:31,36; 25:31,41; 26:53; 28:2,5; Mark 1:13; 8:38; 12:25; 13:37,32; Luke 1:11-19,26-38; 2:9-15,21; 4:10; 9:26, 12:8f; 15:10; 16:22; 20:36; 22:43; 24:23; John 1:51; 5:4; 12:29; 20:12.

The Book of Acts: 5:19; 6:15; 7:30-38,53; 8:26; 10:3,7,22; 11:13; 12:7-15,22; 23:8f; 27:23.

The Epistles: Rom 8:38; 1Cor 4:9; 6:3; 11:10; 13:1; 2Cor 11:14; Gal 1:8; 3:19; 4:14; Col 2:18; 2Thes 1:7; 1Tim 3:16; 5:21; Heb 1:4-7,13; 2:2-9,16; 12:22; 13:2; 1Peter 1:12; 3:22; 2Peter 2:4,11; Jude 1:6.

The Revelation: 1:1,20; 2:1,8,12,18; 3:1,5,7,14; 5:2,11; 7:1,2,11; 8:2-13; 9:1,11-15; 10:1,5-10; 11:1,15; 12:7-9; 14:6-10,15-19; 15:1,6-8; 16:1-12,17; 17:1,7; 18:1,21; 19:17; 20:1; 21:9,12,17; 22:6-8,16.

2) Relationship of angels to Jesus and humans:

Psalms 8:4; Hebrews 2:7: Humans are "a little lower than the angels."

Hebrews 1:4-8: Jesus is "better" than the angels.

Hebrews 1:14: Angels are "ministering spirits" to God's people.

2Peter 2:11: Angels "are greater in power and might" than humans.

3) Named angels:

Michael: Dan 10:13,21; 12:1; Jude; Rev 12:7.

Gabriel: Dan 8:16; 9:21; Luke 1:19,26.

4) Special kinds of angels:

Cherubim: Exod. 25:20

Seraphim: Isa 6:2

Living creatures (or living beings): Ezek 1:5-6; Rev. 4:6.

5) Functions:

Announce good news: Gen 18:9-10; Luke 1:13,30; 2:8-15.

Warn of coming dangers: Gen 18:16; 19:29; Matt. 2:13.

God's agents in the destruction and judgment of evil: Gen 19:13; 2Sam. 24:16.

Caring for and guiding God's people: Gen 24:7,40; 28:12; 31:11; Ps 91:11-12; Exod 14:19; Heb. 1:14.

Protect and provide for the people of God: Gen 21:17-19; Exod 14:19-20; Dan 3:28; Matt 26:53; Mark 1:13; Luke 22:43; Acts 5:19; 12:6-11.

Demons and the Occult

1) General:

Lev 17:7; 19:26-28; Deut 18:9-14; 2Chr 33:1-9; Zech 10:2.

2) Demonic activities:

Oppose God's purposes: Gen 3:1-5; Exod 12:12; Ps 106:36-38; Isa 14:14; Ezek 28:16; 2Thes 2:3f; Rev 16:14.

Oppress people: Job 1:12-19; Matt 9:32f; 2Cor 4:3f; Gal 3:1-3; 1John 3:8; Jude 4; Rev 9:14-19.

Oppose believers: 1Chron 21:1-8; Matt 16:22f; 1Cor 3:1-4; 7:2; 2Cor 2:5-11; Eph 4:26f; 6:10-12; 1Thes 2:2-18; James 3:14-16; Rev 2:12-14; 18:2,24.

Channeling (spiritualism): Lev 19:31; 20:6; Deut 18:11; 1Sam 28:3-20; 1Chron 10:13f.

Astrology: Deut 4:19; 2Kings 17:15; 23:5; Isa 47:12-15.

Miscellaneous: Dan 10:13,20; John 12:31; Eph 2:1-3; 2Thes 2:8-10.

Limited by God: 1Kings 22:20-38; Ps 78:49; Luke 10:17-19; 1Cor 5:1-5; 1Tim 1:19f.

3) Direct attacks by Satan:

Eve: Gen 3:1-5; 2Cor 11:3; Rev 12:9.

Job: Job 1:6-12; 2:1-7.

David: 1Chron 21:1.

High Priest Joshua: Zech 3:1f.

Jesus: Matt 4:1-11.

Peter: Matt 16:21-23; Luke 22:32.

Judas: Luke 22:3-6; John 13:27.

Unnamed woman: Luke 13:16.

Ananias: Acts 5:3.

Paul: 2Cor 12:7; 1Thes 2:18.

Michael the Archangel: Jude 9.

4) Spiritual warfare:

In the OT: 1-8; 2Kings 17:17f; Ps 74:10; Isa 47:12-21; Jer 14:14; Ezek 28:11-19; Dan 10:10-13.

In the Gospels: Matt 6:13; 12:43-45; 13:18f; 24:23f; 28:18-20; Mark 9:17-29; 16:17; Luke 10:17-20; 11:14-23; John 8:44; 13:2; 17:15.

In Acts: 5:16; 8:7-24; 13:6-12; 16:16-18; 17:16f; 19:13-20; 26:18.

In the Epistles: 2Cor 4:1-6; 10:1-6; 11:1-4,13-15; Eph 2:1-7; 4:25-27; 5:15f; 6:10-20; Col 1:13f; 4:2-6; 2Thes 2:1-12; 1Tim 1:18-20; 4:1-11; 6:11f; 2Tim 1:1-8; 2:24-26; 3:1-17; Heb 2:14-18; 13:9; 1Pet 5:8f; Jam 4:7; 1John 4:4-6; 5:18-21.

In the Revelation: Rev 2:9,13,24; 3:9; 12:9; 13:1-18; 16:14; 20:2,7f.

5) Demonic possession:

Matt 8:16,28-34; 9:32-34; 12:22-29; 17:14-20 Mark 1:21-28,32; 7:25-30; Luke 8:2; 11:14; 13:10-21.

6) Can a Christian be possessed?

Yes:
Gen 31:19,34f; 1Sam 16:14.23; Matt 8:16; Luke 13:11; John 13:2,27; Acts 5:1-3; 8:9-24; 1Cor 2:11; 5:1-13; 10:14-22; 2Cor 10:14-22; 4:3f; 11:3f; 2Cor 12:7f; Eph 4:26f; 6:10-18; 1Thes 2:18; 1Tim 3:6f; 4:1; 1Peter 5:6-8; Peter 2:1-22; 1John 4:1-4.

No:
Matt 6:13; John 12:31; 16:11; 17:15; Acts 26:18; 1Cor 10:21; Col 1:13; 2:14f; 2Thes 3:3; Heb 2:14f; 1John 4:4; Rev 20:1-3.

7) Assured defeat of demonic powers:

In the OT: Gen 3:15; Lev 26:30; 2Kings 22:16f; Jer 10:11; Zeph 2:11.

In the NT: Matt 16:18; John 12:31; 19:30; Rom 8:31-39; 16:20; Col 1:13; 2:13-15; Heb 2:14f; 1Pet 3:21; 1John 3:8; Rev 12:7-12; 19:11-21; 20:1-10.

Bibliography:
Nelson's Illustrated Bible Dictionary (Copyright 1986, Thomas Nelson Publishers), on the PC Study Bible (Seattle: WA: Biblesoft), 1995.

All Scripture references from: *New King James Version*. Nashville, TN: Thomas Nelson Publishers, 1982, unless otherwise indicated.

Angels/ Demons and the Occult: Scripture Study. Contained in the book *Scripture Workbook*. Copyright © 1999-2000 by Gary F. Zeolla of Darkness to Light ministry - http://www.dtl.org

Teaching and Defending the Faith

Scripture Study #11

Teaching the Faith

1) The Faith:
A body of essential doctrines which must be taught and believed:
Gal 1:23; 3:23; Eph 4:13; Phil 1:27; Col 2:6f; 1Tim 1:2; 3:9; 5:8; 6:21; 2Tim 3:8; 4:7; Titus 1:4,13; 3:15; 1Pet 5:9; Jude 3 (see Appendixes #1 and #2).

But must not limit teachings to only essential doctrines:
Matt 28:20; Luke 24:27; Acts 20:27; 2Tim 3:16f.

2) Must teach sound doctrine:
1Tim 1:3-7; 3:2; 4:6,11-16; 5:17; 6:2-5; 2Tim 1:13f; 2:2,14,15,24-26; 3:14-17; 4:2-5; Titus 1:9-13; 2:1,15; 3:8.

3) Need for teachers:
Ezra 7:10; Neh 8:1-12; Matt 5:2; 28:18-20; Luke 6:40; 8:9f; Acts 2:42; 8:30f; 20:27; Rom 12:6f; 1Cor 12:28f; Eph 4:11-14; Phil 3:1; Col 1:28f; 1Tim 3:2; 5:17f; 2Pet 1:12-15; 3:1f.

Alternate view:
1John 2:27 says nobody needs to be taught except by the Holy Spirit.

BUT: In 1John the apostle is combating Gnosticism which taught people needed to learn their "secret knowledge" (Gr. *gnosis*) to be saved. It is the teaching of this supposed *gnosis* John is saying his readers do not need. They are already saved without it (2:12-14).

4) Cautions to potential teachers:
1Cor 12:29; 1Tim 1:5-7; James 3:1; 2Pet 2:12; Jude 10.

5) Ministry Age:
Num 4:1-3; 8:24f; 1Chron 23:24-28; 2Chron 31:17; Ezra 3:8; Luke 3:23; 1Tim 4:12.

Defending the Faith

1) Apologetics:
"That branch of Christian theology which has as its aim the reasoned advocacy of the Christian Faith. It includes both positive arguments for the truth of Christianity and rebuttals of criticisms leveled at it" (Erickson, p.14).

"Apologetics" is derived from the Greek word *apologia* which means "defense" (see 1Peter 3:15).

2) The Use of apologetics is Biblical:

In the OT: Ps 11:3; 19:1-6; Prov 15:28; 22:17-21; Isa 41:21-29; Hos 4:1-6 (cp. Prov 29:18).

In the Gospels and Acts: Matt 6:25-34; 10:16; 22:15-46; Luke 1:1-4; John 13:19; Acts 6:3,8-10; 7:1-60; 9:22,29; 17:2-4,10-12,16-34; 18:19,24-28; 19:8f; 23:6-10; 24:10-25; 26:1-29.

In the Epistles: Rom 1-8; 1Cor 9:19-22; 15:1-58; Gal 3:1-29; Phil 1:17; Col 4:5f; 1Pet 3:15; Jude 3.

3) Knowledge of non-Christian religions:

Acts 17:22-31:

In this sermon, Paul confronts several beliefs of Grecian mythology. And note his quotations of two Grecian philosophers in verse 28.

Knowledge of Gnosticism:

Titus 1:12; Col 1:19; 2:9,20-23; 3:5; 1John 1:1,8-2:4,15-17,27; 3:3; 4:1-3; 5:10-13; 2John 7: In these verses Paul and John, respectively, are contradicting specific teachings of Gnosticism.

Acts 26:24:

Paul is known for having "much learning."

4) Arguments against using apologetics:

1Cor 2:1-5:

Paul failed in his attempt to use apologetics in Athens. So he reverted to preaching only Christ in Corinth and depended on miracles to prove his message was true.

BUT: Paul did NOT fail in Athens (Acts 17:34). Further, no miracles are mentioned in the record of Paul's ministry in Corinth in Acts 18. Also, preaching "in Spirit and in power" is not a reference to miracles. John the Baptist's ministry is described in the same way, but he did no miracles (Luke 1:17; John 10:41). In addition, Paul "reasoned" with and "persuaded" the Corinthians (Acts 18:4,12f).

Matt 10:19,20:

We do not have to prepare ourselves with apologetical knowledge. The Holy Spirit will give us what to say when witnessing.

BUT: This passage is not discussing evangelism but dealing with persecution (v.17). And note v.16; we are told to be "wise as serpents" (cp. Prov 15:28).

5) Purpose of miracles:

Exod 4:1-9; 1Kings 17:23f; Mark 16:19f; John 3:2; 5:36; 20:30f; Acts 2:22,43; 2Cor 12:12; Heb 2:4.

6) Miracles don't necessarily cause conversions:

Exod 7-11; Numb 14:11; 1Kings 19:1f; Matt 21:14f; 28:11-15; Luke 16:31; John 2:23-25; 9:13-34; 11:45-53; 12:9-11,37-41; Acts 4:14-22.

7) General approaches:

Prov 18:13,15,17,19; Jer 26:2; Matt 20:19f; Luke 2:46f; 14:1-6; Acts 17:22-31; 20:25-27; Rom 4:4,13f; 11:6; 2Cor 4:5; 1Tim 1:3f; 2Tim 2:23-26; 4:2; 2Pet 3:14-18.

8) DARKNESS TO LIGHT!

Acts 26:18.

In the OT: Ps 18:28; 43:3f; 82:5; Prov 4:18f; Isa 5:20; 8:20; 50:10; 9:2; 35:5; 58:10; 59:2f; 60:1-3,19; Dan 2:22.

In the NT: Luke 1:79; 2:29-31; 11:35; John 1:5-7; 3:19-21; 8:12; 12:35f,46; Rom 2:29; 13:11-14; 2Cor 4:1-6; 6:14; Eph 5:8-11; Col 1:12f; 1Thes 5:4-8; 1Pet 2:9; 1John 1:5-7.

Note:
All Scripture references from: *The New King James Version*. Nashville, TN: Thomas Nelson Publishers, 1982, unless otherwise indicated.

Teaching and Defending the Faith: Scripture Study. Contained in the book *Scripture Workbook*. Copyright © 1999-2000 by Gary F. Zeolla of Darkness to Light ministry - http://www.dtl.org

Controversial Theologies

"Therefore I testify to you this day that I am innocent of the blood of all men. For I have not shunned to declare to you the whole counsel of God" (Acts 20:26,27).

The Sovereignty of God

Scripture Study #12

There are three different professedly Christian viewpoints regarding the sovereignty of God:

Calvinism:
God can and does control human will (or volition, i.e. our individual, personal choices in life). As such, God is absolute Lord over human history in general and individual destinies.

Arminianism:
God could control the human will but chooses not to do so. God is Lord over human history in general, but the destiny of any particular person is determined by the exercise of his or her own "free will."

Pelagianism, Process Theology:
God is incapable of controlling human will. As such, He is not Lord over human history nor over personal destinies. Human "free-will" or "chance" are the ultimate determinate factors. But God is doing the best He can to bring about good in the world.

Studying the following passages will help the reader to decide which of the above positions is the most Biblical. Whatever position is taken, one thing should become clear: the concept of the sovereignty of God pervades the Scriptures.

In the Life of Joseph:

Gen 37:5-11 (cp. 42:6-9; 43:26-28); 37:18-28,36; 39:1-5; 20-23; 41:25-32; 42:28; 43:14; 45:4-8; 50:18-20; Ps 105:16f.

In the Exodus:

Exod 3:21; 4:21; 6:1-8; 7:3-5,19-21; 8:6-24,31; 9:1-6,12,22-29; 10:12-15,19-23,27; 11:3-9; 12:29f,35f,40f (cp. Gen 15:13f); 13:19 (cp. Gen 50:24f); 14:4-8,15-31; 15:1-21.

Elsewhere in the Torah:

Gen 20:1-6; 31:1-16,42; 35:5 (cp. 34:30); 38:7-10.

Exod 4:11 (Does God merely "permit" birth defects or does He CAUSE them? What does this verse teach?); 21:12f; 23:27; 34:23f; 35:3-36:2.

Lev 14:34.

Numb 11:31; 23:19.

Deut 2:24-33 (cp. Numb 21:21-24); 3:18-22; 11:25 (cp. Josh 6:1); 20:1-4 (cp. Exod 17:8-11); 28:1-68; 29:2-4; 32:39.

In the Life of David:

1Sam 17:37,45-47; 18:10-14; 23:24-29; 26:10 (cp. 31:1-6); 26:12.

2Sam 5:17-25; 8:6,14; 12:7-11 (cp. 15:16; 16:20-22); 12:14f; 15:25f,31-34; 16:5-12; 17:5-7,14; 18:19,28; 21:1,14; 22:1-23:12; 24:1-15,25.

1Chr 10:13f; 11:14; 12:16-18; 14:2,10-17; 22:11-13.

In the Kingdoms of Israel and Judah:

1Kings 5:12; 8:33-61; 9:4-9; 11:14,23,31f; 12:15,21; 13:20-30; 14:14 (cp. 15:25-30); 17:17-22; 21:17-21; 22:17f,23,28,34-38.

2Kings 3:9-24; 6:24; 7:1-7,17-20; 8:1-6; 9:30-36; 19:25-28,32-37; 20:1-11; 24:1-4,20.

2Chron 1:1,11f; 2:11f; 11:4; 12:2-12; 13:4-20; 14:6,9-14; 15:6; 16:7-9; 17:3-5,10; 18:22,31-34; 20:1-30,35-37; 20:5-9; 21:10,18,24; 25:8,14-23; 26:5-8,16-21; 27:6; 28:1-6,19; 29:3-11,36; 30:6-9,12; 31:10; 32:7f,13-15,20f,26; 33:1f,9-13; 34:19-28; 35:20-24; 36:11-22.

In the Book of Esther:

Note: No where in Esther is God ever actually mentioned. But can all of the following incidents be solely attributed to "coincidence" or "chance?"

Est 2:17,21-23; 3:5-7; 4:10-17; 5:1-3,14; 6:1-5; 7:7-10 (cp. Gal 6:7); 8:2,15-17; 9:1-5,23-25; 10:1-3 (cp. Matt 20:16).

Elsewhere in OT History:

Josh 1:8-11; 11:19f; 21:43-45; 23:14-16.

Judg 2:13-16; 7:22; 10:7; 11:21; 9:22-24,56f.

Ruth 1:19-21; 4:13-17.

1Sam 2:6-10,25 (cp. 4:11).

Ezra 1:1-5; 6:22; 7:6-10,27f,31; 8:18,21-23 (ct. Neh 2:9); 9:5-9.

Neh 1:7-11; 2:7f,12,17-20; 4:6-20; 6:15f; 7:5; 9:4-38; 12:43; 13:17f (Note the interplay between divine sovereignty and human responsibility in rebuilding the wall and in defending the work from adversaries).

In OT Poetry:

Job 1:8-12; 2:6; 23:1-7; 38:1-42:17 (Job wants his "day in court" to plea his righteousness before God. When that day comes, God rebukes him, and Job repents of his arrogance. The focus of the Book of Job is not the "problem of evil" but the sovereignty of God).

Psalm 2:1-12; 33:6-11; 37:12-15; 44:1-3; 103:19; 105:24f; 110:3; 112:7; 115:3; 139:16 (cp. Acts 17:26).

Prov 16:1,4,33 (cp. Acts 1:23-26); 19:21; 20:24; 21:1,30f; 22:2.

In the Book of Isaiah:

Isa 1:19-26; 2:10-18; 5:26; 8:10,13; 9:8-14,19-21; 10:5-15,20-27,33f; 11:11-16; 13:4,17-22; 14:24-27; 17:12-14; 19:2,11-17; 21:16f; 22:15-23; 25:8; 26:12; 27:1; 31:1-9; 37:7,29,36-38; 38:5-8; 40:6-31; 41:2-4,10-20,25; 42:15-17,24f; 43:9-13; 44:6-8,11-13,23-28; 45:1-13 (cp. Ezra 1:1-5; 6:22); 45:22-25; 46:9-11; 48:3; 49:23f; 50:2f; 51:3,12-16,22f; 52:4-10; 54:16f; 55:6-13; 59:1,18-21; 60:19-22; 61:11; 62:6f; 63:14-17; 64:8; 65:1,8-10; 65:17,25; 66:1f,22f.

In the Writings of Jeremiah:

Jer 1:4-10,13-19; 2:36f; 6:19; 7:3; 11:18-23; 18:5-11; 10:23-25; 23:4-10; 25:8-16,30-33; 29:4,10-14; 30:10f; 31:35; 32:38-42; 34:20-22; 36:26; 40:3; 44:11-13,23-30; 46:15f,25f; 47:6f; 49:2-22; 50:18-46; 51:11,20-23,53.

Lam 1:5,12-18; 2:8,16f,22; 3:37-39; 5:19-22.

In OT Prophecy:

Ezek 5:11-17; 23:23-30; 29:19f; 30:10-12.

Dan 1:9,17-20; 2:19-23,28-30,37; 3:10-30; 4:2f,17,25-37; 5:17-31; 6:16-31; 7:21f,27; 9:24-27.

Hos 2:7-18.

Joel 2:25; 3:2-8.

Amos 3:6; 4:6-13; 5:8f; 6:8,14; 9:2-6.

Obad 1-4.

Jonah 1:4,7,14-17; 2:10; 4:6-8.

Micah 1:3f,12; 2:7,12f; 4:6f,9-13; 6:13.

Nahum 1:3-8; 2:13.

Hab 1:5f; 3:1-19.

Zeph 1:2-18; 2:11; 3:6,9,14-17.

Hag 1:7-11,14; 2:4-8,17-23.

Zech 1:5f; 2:13; 4:6; 12:1,10; 14:12-19.

Mal 1:2-5,11-14; 2:1; 4:1-6.

In the Messiah's Death:

(God determined the time and manner of the Messiah's death, not the Jews or the Romans.)

Matt 26:1-5,17,51-56.

Luke 4:28-30; 22:22.

John 7:30; 8:20,59; 10:31-33,39 (cp. Ps 22:14-18); John 18:3-9 (cp. John 17:12; Ps 41:9); 18:31f (cp. John 3:14; 8:28; 12:32f); 19:6-16,23f,31-38.

Acts 2:22-24; 4:27f; 13:29.

Eph 1:7-12; 3:10f.

1Peter 1:17-21.

Rev 13:7f.

In the Book of Acts:

Acts 5:33-42; 8:4,26-40; 12:20-24; 13:48; 16:6f,25-34; Acts 17:24-26; 18:9f; 23:11; 27:22-26,39-44; 28:1-10,16,30f.

Elsewhere in the NT:

Matt 8:28-32; 10:29; Rom 8:28-30; 2Cor 8:16; Eph 1:3-14; 3:11; Phil 2:12f; 1Thes 3:11-13; 5:18; 2Thes 2:8; 3:5; 2Tim 2:7; 3:10f; 4:16-18; Jam 4:13-15; Rev 11:15-19; 17:15-17; 19:6,11-21; 21:1-8,22-27.

Over our Senses:

Gen 21:19; Exod 4:11 (cp. John 9:1-3); Ps 94:9; Prov 20:12; 29:13; 2Kings 6:15-17; Luke 24:16,31.

Over the Weather:

Gen 41:25-31; Exod 9:26; Deut 28:12,23f; 1Kings 8:35f; 2Chr 7:13f; Job 38:25-38; Ps 107:25,29; 135:7; 147:8,15-18; 148:8; Isa 5:6; 30:23; Jer 3:2f; 5:23-25; 14:22; 51:15f; Amos 4:7f; Jonah 1:4,12-16; 4:8; Hag 1:7-11; Zech 14:17-19; Matt 5:45; Mark 4:35-41; Acts 14:17; Jam 5:17f.

Over Conception/ Pregnancy:

Gen 4:4; 18:9-15 (cp. 21:1f); 20:17f; 25:21; 29:31; 30:22; 31:7-9; 1Chr 25:5; Neh 9:23; Ps 127:3; Isa 44:2,24; Hos 9:14; Luke 1:8-25.

In the Inspiration of Scripture:

2Sam 23:2; Isa 1:20; 40:5; 58:14; 59:21; Luke 1:70; Mark 12:36; Acts 1:16; 2Tim 3:16f; Heb 1:1; 2Pet 1:21.

Since God is Truth (Deut 32:4; John 3:33) and cannot lie (Numb 23:19; Titus 1:2), all His words are true and perfectly reliable (2Sam 7:28; Ps 19:7; 93:5; John 17:17; Rev 21:5).

Note: All Scripture references from: *The New King James Version.* Nashville, TN: Thomas Nelson Publishers, 1982, unless otherwise indicated.

The Sovereignty of God: Scripture Study. Contained in the book *Scripture Workbook.* Copyright © 1999-2000 by Gary F. Zeolla of Darkness to Light ministry - http://www.dtl.org

The Five Points of Calvinism

Scripture Study #13

Calvinism:
A system of theology deriving its name from the reformer John Calvin (1509-1564). It emphasizes the sovereignty of God in predestining and electing some to salvation, based solely upon His free and unmerited favor. Calvinism is often expressed by the acronym TULIP:

T: Total Depravity:
The intellect, will, and emotions are corrupted by sin in every person. This doctrine does not teach we are as bad as we could possibly be. It means that do due to our corrupt nature we are unable, of ourselves, to turn to Christ to be saved. Further, we all sin and even our "good" acts are tainted by impure motives (also called Radical Corruption).

In the OT: Gen 6:5; 8:21; Num 15:37-39; 1Ki 8:46; Job 15:14-16; Ps 14:1-3; 51:5; 94:11; 130:3; Pr 4:23; 20:9; Eccl 7:20; 8:11; Isa 6:5; 53:6; 64:6f; Jer 10:14; 13:23; 17:9.

In the Gospels and Acts: Matt 7:11; 15:19; Mark 10:18; Luke 17:10; John 2:24f; 3:36; 6:44; 15:5,16; Acts 3:16; 16:14.

In the Epistles and the Revelation: Rom 1:18-2:16; 3:9-20,23; 5:12; 7:18-20; 8:7f; 1Cor 2:14; 12:3; 2Cor 3:5; 4:3f; 11:3; Eph 2:1-6; 4:17-19; Col 2:13; 1Tim 2:25; 6:5; 2Tim 3:8; Titus 1:5; Jam 2:10; 3:2,8; Rev 9:20f; 16:9.

U: Unconditional Election:

God's choice of certain persons to salvation is not dependent upon any foreseen virtue or faith on their part.

In the OT: Deut 7:6-10,15; 9:5; 29:4; Ps 65:4; Isa 45:4.

In the Gospels and Acts: Mark 13:20; John 1:13; 6:44,65; 15:16; 17:2; Acts 2:39; 9:1-18; 11:17f; 16:14; 18:27.

In the Epistles and the Revelation: Rom 8:28-30; 9:10-26; 10:20; 11:5; Eph 1:1-11; 1Cor 1:1; 2Cor 4:6; Phil 1:29; 1Thes 1:2-4; 2Thes 2:13; 2Tim 1:9; 2:10,19,25f; Titus 3:5; Heb 9:15; James 1:18; Jude 1.

L: Limited Atonement:

Christ's atoning death was effectual only for the elect. These are those whom God, by His grace, chose to be His own from eternity past. Christ's death truly and actually propitiated God's wrath against them. The rest are justly damned for their sins (also called Particular or Specific Redemption).

In the OT: Exod 4:21; 14:4,8,17; Deut 2:30; 9:4-7; 29:4; Josh 11:19f; 1Sam 2:25; 3:14; 2Sam 17:14; Ps 105:25; Pr 15:8f,26; 28:9; Isa 53:11; Jer 24:7.

In the Gospels and Acts: Matt 1:21; 11:25-27; 13:10-15,44-46; 15:13: 20:28; 22:14; 24:22; Luke 8:15; 13:23f; 19:42; John 5:21; 6:37,44,65; 8:42-47; 10:11,14f,26-28; 11:49-53; 12:37-41; 13:1,18; 15:16; 17:2,6,9; 18:9,37; Acts 2:39; 13:48; 18:27; 19:9.

In the Epistles and the Revelation: Rom 9:10-26; 11:5-10; 1Cor 1:18-31; 2:14f; 2Cor 2:14-16; 4:3f; Gal 1:3f; Eph 2:1-10; Col 2:13f; 2Thes 2:9-14; 2Tim 2:20,25; Titus 2:14; Heb 1:3,14; 2:9f,16f (cp. Gal 3:29; 4:28-31); 9:28; 1Pet 2:8; 2Pet 2:7f; 1John 4:6; Jude 1,14; Rev 13:8; 17:8,15-18; 21:27.

I: Irresistible Grace:

All those whom God has chosen for eternal life will come to faith (also called Effectual Grace). The related issue of God's sovereignty over people in general is also reflected in the following verses. For additional verses on this subject see "The Sovereignty of God" (Scripture Study #12).

In the OT: Gen 20:6; 35:5; Exod 34:23f; Deut 2:25; 30:6; Judg 14:1-4; 1Ki 4:29; 1Chr 22:12; 29:18f; Ezra 1:1,5; 6:22; 7:27f; Neh 1:11; 2:8,12; Est 2:17; 4:14; 6:1-4; Ezek 36:25-32; Ps 33:10f; 65:4; 139:16; Pr 21:1; Isa 44:28; Jer 10:24; Hag 1:14.

In the NT: Luke 24:16,31,45; John 6:37,45; 10:3,4,27; Acts 11:18; 13:48; 16:14; 17:26; 1Cor 3:5f; 12:13; 15:10; 2Cor 8:16; Gal 2:8; Eph 2:1-6; 3:7; Phil 2:13; Heb 13:20; Jam 4:13-15.

P: Perseverance of the Saints:

Genuine believers will persevere in the way of holiness until glorification. This doctrine does not teach believers can attain sinlessness in this life, but a true believer's life will be characterized by ever increasing holiness. The Holy Spirit will convict believers when they sin and lead them back to the path of righteousness (also called Eternal Security).

In the OT: 1Sam 2:9; Neh 9:16-19; Ps 31:23; 32:7,23f,28-33,38f; 84:5-7; 89:30-33; 94:14; 97:10; 97:10; 121:7f; 125:1f; Prov 2:8; Isa 40:30f; 54:4-10; Jer 32:38-42.

In the Gospels: Matt 18:6.12-14; 24:22-24; Luke 1:74f; 22:32; John 3:36; 4:13f; 5:24; 6:37-40,51; 8:31; 10:4f,8,27-29; 17:11f,15.

In the Epistles: Rom 6:1-4; 7:24-8:4,28-39; 11:29; 14:14; 1Cor 1:4-9; 3:15; 10:13; 2Cor 1:22; 5:5; Eph 1:11-14; 4:30 Phil 1:6; Col 3:1-4; 1Thes 5:23; 2Thes 3:3-5; 2Tim 1:12; 4:18; Heb 3:14; 7:25; 10:14,36-39; 13:5f; 1Pet 1:3-5; 2Pet 3:8f; 1John 2:19; 3:9; 5:4f,13,18; Jude 1,24.

Bibliography: The above definitions are adapted from: Criswell, W.A. ed. *The Believer's Study Bible: NKJV.* Nashville: Thomas Nelson, 1991.

Erickson, Millard. *Concise Dictionary of Christian Theology.* Grand Rapids: Baker, 1986.

All Scripture references from: *The New King James Version.* Nashville, TN: Thomas Nelson Publishers, 1982, unless otherwise indicated.

Arminian Arguments Against the Five Points of Calvinism:

with Rebuttals

Scripture Study #14

Note:
In this study, the argument an Arminian would raise against one of The Five Points of Calvinism is presented immediately below each Scripture reference.(1) After the "BUT" is the rebuttal to the argument.

Genesis 6:5,6; Ezekiel 33:11:
God is hurt by our actions, so He can't be in control of our destinies.

BUT: Even though God is Spirit (John 4:24), He is often spoken of in physical terms (Isa 37:17; 45:12; 51:5). This is done as an aid to our finite minds in comprehending the infinite God. In the same way, God is said to be "grieved" by our actions to help us understand His moral nature and standards (Ezek 33:1-10).

Deuteronomy 30:19,20; Joshua 24:15:
An offer of choice implies the freedom and ability to choose.

BUT: People with "totally depraved " natures, left to themselves, choose to reject the true God because He does not appeal to them (Rom 1:18-24). When God, by His grace, changes the nature of His elect, they choose to come to Him because they now desire Him (Ps 73:25-28).

Psalm 69:28:

"Let them be blotted out of the book of life" indicates people can lose their salvation.

BUT: A better way of translating the verse would be, "Let them be blotted out of the book of the living" (NKJV see also KJV). The reason this is a better translation is "living" in Hebrew is an adjective, not a noun. Thus, David is not praying for his enemies to be eternally damned; he is simply asking for them to be killed (i.e. to be no longer among the "living [ones]").

The preceding context further confirms this interpretation (verses 22-27). Throughout these verses, David is praying for temporal judgments to come upon his enemies; eternity is not being discussed. The "salvation" David is asking for in verse 29 is salvation from his enemies, not eternal salvation. The Psalm simply doesn't have eternity in view, but temporal concerns.

Isaiah 53:6:

Christ died for "all" people.

BUT: "All" in this verse does not refer to every person who has or will live. It refers only to those whom will have "peace" with God (v.5).

Ezekiel 18:24,32:

If a righteous person turns from his righteousness he will die. So people can loose their salvation. And God has "no pleasure in the death of one who dies."

BUT: "die" in Ezekiel 18 does not mean "damnation" just as "live" does not mean eternal life. The chapter is discussing temporal rewards and punishments, not the eternal state. It is directed towards the "house of Israel" and concerns its current "Babylonian captivity" and the coming Babylonian destruction of Jerusalem (v.31).

The people are claiming their captivity and the coming destruction are due to their ancestors' sins, not their own (v.2). Ezekiel is correcting their misconception and telling them that they are being judged for their own sins (v.4). But God will relent if they "repent and turn from their transgressions" (v.30).

Matthew 25:41:
"Then He will also say to those on the left hand, 'Depart from Me, you cursed, into the everlasting fire prepared for the devil and his angels.'" No human being was predestinated for hell. It was not created for people. It was prepared for the devil and his angels.

BUT: It doesn't say prepared ONLY for the Devil and his angels. Jesus is just indicating that the lost will be in the same place as the Devil.

Furthermore, in the Sublapsarian, Calvinist view (which most Calvinists ascribed to), the logical order of decrees is: creation, the fall of Satan, the Fall of humanity, then the predestination of human beings. So in the logical order of events, Hell was initially created "only" for Satan and his angels, but then after the Fall God predestined the reprobate to go there as well.

John 1:29; 3:16; 4:42:
Christ "takes away the sin of the world," God loves the "world" and Jesus is "Savior of the world." So the atonement is universal, not limited.

BUT: "world" (Gr. *kosmon*) does not necessarily mean everyone living on the entire earth (Luke 2:1; John 1:10; 7:4,7; Acts 17:6; Rom 1:8).

John 3:16:

"whosoever" can believe.

BUT: "whosoever" is not the best rendering of the Greek phrase used here (*pas o pisteuon*). A literal translation would be "everyone believing" (see the ALT and LITV).

John 12:32:

Christ will draw "all peoples" to Himself.

BUT: "Peoples" (NKJV) or "men" (KJV) is not in the Greek. It simply says "all" (*pas*). For a discussion on this word, see 1Timothy 2:3,4 below. Also, Jesus teaches that one first has to be "drawn" (Gr. *elkuse*) by the Father to come to Him (John 6:44 and cp. Acts 21:20; James 2:6 where the same word is translated "drag" in the NKJV).

Romans 8:29-30:

"For whom He foreknew, He also predestined to be conformed to the image of His Son, that He might be the firstborn among many brethren." Predestination was based on God's foreknowledge of who would believe. Moreover, the predestination is not to salvation but to be conformed to Christ.

BUT: It does not say predestination was based on God's foreknowledge. The text simply says that whom He foreknew He "also" predestined. So the text is asserting two points that are simultaneous, not saying one is dependant on the other.

Moreover, the text does not say those whom He foreknew WOULD BELIEVE.... Those last two words are being read into the text. The question is, what is meant by "foreknew?" It could be "whom He foreknew THAT HE WOULD SAVE" which would make sense given the next words, "He also predestinated to be conformed to the image of his Son." So the verse is teaching God predestined that His elect would be conformed to Christ.

2Corinthians 3:16:

The "veil" is taken away after one turns to the Lord, so people are capable of turning to God on their own.

BUT: The "veil" being removed is one of misunderstanding the Scriptures (v.14). The question still remains, how do people turn to the Lord in the first place? (see v.5).

Ephesians 1:5:

"having predestined us to adoption as sons by Jesus Christ to Himself, according to the good pleasure of His will"--it's "us" (the saved) who are predestinated, to "adoption."

BUT: It's us "the elect" who are predestined to "adoption." The needed words are added in either case. But note the words in the previous verse, "He chose us in Him before the foundation of the world." That sounds like election and why "the elect" fits better in verse five than "the saved."

Ephesians 1:11:

"In Him also we have obtained an inheritance, being predestined according to the purpose of Him who works all things according to the counsel of His will"--it is the inheritance we are predestined to, not salvation.

BUT: This verse is near the end of the long sentence of Eph 1:3-14. So it's a package. The main subject is "He chose us in Him (v.4)." So "inheritance" is not the antecedent of "predestined." And even if it is, what is the "inheritance" but "something" associated with salvation?

1Timothy 2:3,4:

God desires "all" to be saved.

BUT: "all" (Gr. *pas*) in Scripture does not necessarily mean every person on the face of the earth (Matt 3:5f; 10:22; John 3:26; Col 1:23). Paul uses the word 22 other times in 1Timothy and in many of these references it does not refer to "all existing examples of" something but rather "all kinds of" something or some other meaning (1Tim 1:15; 2:1,2,6,8,11; 3:4,11; 4:4,8,9,10,15; 5:2,10,20; 6:1,10,13,17).

Particularly pertinent is 6:10, "For the love of money is the root of all evil" (KJV). Money was not the "root" of Satan's rebellion, or of the Fall of Adam and Eve, or of many other sins. However, money is "a root of all kinds of evil" (NKJV; note: There is no definitive article "the" in the Greek text of this verse).

Similarly "all" in 1Tim 2:4 does not refer to every person who has or will live. It refers to all kinds of people as opposed to only Jews (cp. Matt 13:47; Acts 10:34f; 11:18; Rev 5:9). Moreover, if God wanted every person to be saved, then everyone would be saved since His will always comes to pass (Isa 55:11; Ps 33:10; 115:3; 135:6). But the Bible clearly teaches some will be damned (Matt 25:26; Rev 20:11-15; 21:8).

Titus 2:11:
"For the grace of God that brings salvation has appeared to all men." So God's grace is available to everyone.

BUT: Note the "For" at the beginning of the verse. This conjunction means this verse is an explanation of what has preceded. The preceding verses are injunctions to Christians on how we should live. It is only Christians who are looking forward to the Second Coming (v.13). Thus "all men" refers to "all Christians" (see discussion on "all" for 1Tim 2:3,4 above).

Hebrews 2:9:

Christ tasted "death for everyone." So the atonement is universal.

BUT: "one" is not in the Greek. The word is *pas* which means "all" or "every." (see the MKJV, LITV, or ALT). But "all" of whom? Verse 10 begins with "For" which means the following verses will explain the previous ones. In these verses the writer refers to "sons" (v.10), "brethren" (vv.11,17), "children" (vv.14,15), and "the seed of Abraham" (vv.16). These terms best describe "those who are of faith," not people in general (see Gal 3:6-16).

Hebrews 6:4-6:

A description of true believers who are in danger of loosing their salvation.

BUT: Everything said in this passage could apply to Judas (Mark 3:13-19; 6:7-13), Simon the Sorcerer (Acts 8:13-17), and the people in Matt 7:21-23. But it is very doubtful any of these ever genuinely believed (John 17:12; Acts 8:21, and note the word "never" in Matt 7:23). Also, the writer believes the recipients will do "things that accompany salvation" (Heb 6:9). One of these "things" is perseverance (Heb 3:14; 1John 2:19).

2Peter 2:1:

The false prophets are "denying the Lord who bought them" so Jesus died even for unbelievers.

BUT: This verse is not discussing the atonement of Christ. 1Peter was written to Jewish Christians. So it is probable that 2Peter was also (1Pet 1:1; cp. Gal 2:7f). To the unbelieving Jews among the Jewish Christians, "the Lord" would most naturally refer to God the Father, not Jesus. And all Jews were "bought" by God in the Exodus.

2Peter 2:20-22:

People escape "the pollutions of the world" and then return to them.

BUT: Notice, the text simply says they have "known the way of righteousness" (v.21). There is no mention of belief or salvation. And the "dog" and "sow" return to their old ways (v.22). They never ceased to be dogs or sows.

2Peter 3:9:

God is "not willing that any should perish but that all should come to repentance."

BUT: "any" or "all" of what? Dogs? Chickens? There must be an antecedent to the pronouns. In 3:3-7, Peter is discussing "them" (i.e. unbelievers). In verse 8 he addresses the "beloved." The beloved are those to whom the epistle is addressed, "those who have obtained a like precious faith with us" (1:1). Thus, God is not will willing that any of the BELOVED should perish. And, since God gets everything He wants, this verse becomes a proof-text for eternal security.

Moreover, the context of this passage is when the end of the world will come (3:7,10). Peter is teaching that God will wait until "all" have a chance to repent. If "all" refers to everyone who has lived or will live, then the world would never end as new people are being born all the time!

But if the reference is to all of God's people, then the world will end when the last of the elect (a large but finite number) has repented and believed. Or, since the epistle most likely was written to Jewish Christians (see on 2Peter 2:1 above), then the reference is to the elect among the Jews, and the world will end when the last elect Jew has repented.

1John 2:2:

Jesus died for the sins of "the whole world" not just the elect.

BUT: In 5:19 John writes, "the whole world lies under the sway of the evil one." But "the whole world" here cannot include believers (4:4). Thus, "the whole world" only includes all of a certain class of people. 5:19 refers to the class of the lost; 2:2 to the class of the elect.

Revelation 2:7:

Only those who "overcome" will ultimately be saved.

BUT: John declares in his first epistle, "who is he who overcomes the world, but he who believes Jesus is the Son of God" (1John 5:5).

Revelation 22:17:

"whosoever desires" is called to salvation.

BUT: A literal translation of the Greek phrase *o thelon* would be, "the one desiring" (see the LITV). And the main issue still remains, where does this desire initially come from, within the person or from God? The desire and ability to repent and believe in Christ cannot come from within our own sinful natures (Jer 13:23; Rom 8:7f; 1Cor 2:14; 12:3). So it must come from God! (John 6:44).

As Luke writes,
"And as many as had been appointed to eternal life believed"
(Acts 13:48).

Note:

1) An Arminian is one who ascribes to the theological system developed by Jacob Arminius (1560-1609). The Five Points of Calvinism were originally drafted to contradict the basic teachings of Arminianism.

119

Questions on Baptism

Scripture Study #15

Notes: After each question, the answer(s) which Darkness to Light ministry disagrees with are given first. Below each Scripture reference is how "the other side" interprets the verse. After the "BUT" is the reason this ministry disagrees with that interpretation. Then the answer this ministry would give to the question is given, followed by Scripture verses and interpretations thereof. In the parentheses following each answer is a sample of groups adhering to that position.

Is Baptism Necessary for Salvation?

Yes (Catholicism, Mormonism, Churches of Christ):

Matthew 3:13-15:
Jesus was baptized, so it must be important.

BUT: Important yes, but this does not mean it is necessary for salvation; Jesus did not need to be saved!

Mark 16:16:
People who believe and are baptized are saved.

BUT: The textual difficulty of Mark 16:9-20 makes this passage a precarious proof-text. But accepting it as genuine, two kinds of people are mentioned, "He who believes and is baptized" and "he who does not believe." The third possibility, "He who believes but is not baptized" is not mentioned. So this passage proves nothing in this regard.

John 3:5:

Jesus says people must be born of water and the Spirit.

BUT: Baptism is not actually mentioned. "Water" could be referring to many other things: the cleansing properties of the Word of God (John 15:3 Eph 5:26; 1Pet 1:23); "the washing of regeneration and renewing of the Holy Spirit" (Titus 3:5; see also Ezek 36:25); suffering (Matt 10:38, cp. Isa 43:1f, "water" in the Septuagint is singular).

Most likely, it refers to the waters of natural birth. Note the parallel between "born of water" with "born of the flesh" in the next verse (cp. John 1:12f). In any case, in John 3:6-8 only the Spirit is mentioned as being involved in regeneration.

Acts 2:38:

Peter tells people to be baptized for the remission of sins.

BUT: The commands of "repent" and "be baptized" in Acts 2:38 have different grammatical forms so they are not both linked with "the remission of sins." The word "repent" is a second-person, plural, active imperative. The words "be baptized" translate a third-person, singular, passive imperative. So the phrase with the words "be baptized" is a parenthetical comment.

On the other hand, in Acts 3:19, the verbs "repent" and "be converted" do have the same grammatical forms. But baptism is not mentioned. So baptism is to be submitted to AFTER repentance and conversion.

Or, the Greek word "for" can also mean "because of." The same word is used in Matt 3:11 where people were baptized by John BECAUSE OF their repentance (see also Matt 12:41 where "at" is again the same word).

Acts 22:16:
Sins are "washed away" in baptism.

BUT: "calling" is a participle and should be taken in an instrumental sense; i.e. "wash away your sins BY calling on the name of the Lord" (see the ALT, and cp. Acts 2:21).

Titus 3:5:
"washing of regeneration" is a reference to baptism and is separate from the "renewing of the Holy Spirit."

BUT: The two are not necessarily separate. But even it they are, the text does not specifically equate "water of regeneration" with baptism. See on John 3:5 above for other possibilities of what this "water" could be referring to.

Hebrews 10:22:
Our hearts are "sprinkled from an evil conscience."

BUT: Baptism is not specifically mentioned. The allusion is to a passage like Lev 16:14-17 where BLOOD, not water, was sprinkled on people. This ritual symbolized Christ's coming blood sacrifice that would cleanse sins (Acts 20:28; 1Pet 1:18f).

1Peter 3:21:
Peter says baptism saves us.

BUT: He specifically says that what saves is "the answer of a good conscience towards God" (cp. Heb 9:14).

No (Most Protestant denominations and churches):

John 3:16; 6:28,29; 20:31:

By "believing" we can have life in Christ. No mention is made of baptism (cp. 1John 5:13).

Luke 23:39-43:

The thief on the cross will be "in Paradise" with Jesus without having been baptized.

Acts 10:44-48:

The Holy Spirit "fell upon" and was "poured out" on Cornelius and those with him and "received" by them; they "speak with tongues and magnify God" all BEFORE being baptized. So baptism cannot be necessary to receive the Holy Spirit (cp. Luke 11:13). And having the Spirit is the mark of being saved (Rom 8:9-11).

Romans 2:28,29; Gal 5:6; 6:13-15:

Paul's words about circumcision in these verses could easily apply to baptism. Outward ceremonies do not change a person but the Spirit working in a person's heart. Further, faith and love are what are important in the Christian life. Outward ceremonies "avail nothing." What matters is being "a new creation" in Christ Jesus (cp. 2Cor 5:17).

Romans 4:11,12:

Again, Paul's words about circumcision could easily apply to baptism. Abraham was saved BEFORE he was circumcised. Circumcision was only a "sign" of the righteousness he had previously received by faith (see Rom 4:3).

1Corinthians 1:14-17:

Paul declares, "For Christ did not send me to baptize, but to preach the gospel." So he separates the Gospel from baptism. Also, baptism is so much of a concern to Paul that he can't even remember whom he baptized!

Ephesians 2:8-10:

Baptism is a work, but we are saved by grace. However, being baptized is one of the "good works which God prepared beforehand" that we should engage in after being saved.

1Peter 1:23:

"the word of God" is the outward agent in our regeneration, not water.

Who Should Be Baptized?

Infants (Catholicism, Lutheranism, Reformed/ Presbyterian churches):

Acts 16:14,15,31-33:

"Households" are baptized which surely included children.

BUT: This is a big assumption. Infants and children are not mentioned.

Colossians 2:11,12:

Baptism is equated with circumcision which was performed on infants. In the same way, infants should now be baptized.

BUT: The passage does not necessary connect baptism with circumcision. And besides, Paul is referring to both in a metaphorical sense ("made without hands" - cp. Rom 2:28f).

Believers only (Baptists, Mennonites, Pentecostals/ Charismatics):

Acts 2:41; 8:12,35-38; 9:18; 10:44-48; 18:8; 19:1-7:
In all of these cases people exercise faith in Christ before being baptized. Infants are incapable of trusting Christ. And in none of these passages are infants mentioned.

How Should a Person Be Baptized?

By sprinkling (Pedobaptist churches; i.e. churches that baptize infants. "pedo" comes from the Greek word for child.):

Matthew 3:11:
People are baptized "with" water.

BUT: The Greek word is only rarely translated as "with." Much more often it is translated as "in" (see the ALT).

Acts 2:41:
Only by sprinkling could the twelve apostles baptize 3000 people in one day. Also, there are not sufficient water sources in Jerusalem to immerse 3000 people.

BUT: It was probably not only the twelve apostles, but others from the 120 who had been praying in the upper room who helped in the baptizing (Acts 1:15; 2:10). 3000 divided by 120 equals only 25 baptisms each. And note, they started early in the day (Acts 2:15; "the third hour" would be 9:00 am).

As for the water, some could have traveled the 20 miles to the Jordan River by horse or camelback. Others could have been baptized in closer streams, public and private baths, or other sources of water.

One way or another, the logistics could have been worked out. Remember the apostles had previously fed "about five thousand men, besides women and children" and gathered up the leftovers in one day. And then they did not start until "it was evening" (Matt 14:14-21). They later did the same for "four thousand men, besides women and children" (Matt 15:38). So the disciples were not new to organizing large crowds on the spur of the moment.

Hebrews 10:22:
"having our hearts sprinkled" is a reference to baptism.

BUT: Baptism isn't actually mentioned. And even if this verse is a reference to baptism, the second half of the verse adds "our bodies washed with pure water." It is difficult to wash an entire body by "sprinkling" it!

By pouring (Pedobaptist churches, most Mennonite churches):

Acts 2:17; Titus 3:5,6:
Baptism should be by pouring to symbolize the reception of the Holy Spirit by the believer.

BUT: Baptism is not specifically mentioned in these verses. And see above on Titus 3:5.

By immersion (Baptists, Mennonite Brethren, Pentecostals/ Charismatics):

Matthew 3:5,6; John 3:23:
John baptized at the Jordan river because he needed "much water."

Matthew 3:11:

The word "baptize" is just a transliteration of the Greek word. The meaning of the word is "immerse" (see the ALT).

Matthew 3:16; Acts 8:38,39:

They "went down into the water" and "came up out of the water."

Romans 6:3-6:

Baptism is a symbolic representation of believers dying to their old lives, being buried with Christ, and rising to new lives in Christ. To symbolize "burial" requires immersion.

Should Believers Be Baptized for the Dead?

Yes (Mormonism):

1Corinthians 15:29:

Paul teaches that believers are to be baptized for the dead.

BUT: The context of this verse is Paul contending with people who deny the resurrection of the dead. Paul is saying that "they" baptize for the dead. The "they" are the heretics. In the next two verses Paul uses the words "we" and "I" thus separating himself and other believers from the "they."

Paul's purpose in citing the practice of the heretics is apologetical, not theological. He is showing that "they" are inconsistent to deny the resurrection of the dead and yet to be engaging in this practice. He is not teaching doctrine.

1Peter 3:19; 4:6:

The Gospel is preached to those who are dead. So we must be baptized for them so they can be saved.

BUT: The verses do not mention baptism. Furthermore, the conclusion makes two assumption, both questionable. First, it assumes baptism is necessary for salvation. But see above for arguments against this position.

Second, the conclusion assumes Peter is teaching there is a "second chance" for salvation after death. But there are other possible interpretations of these verses. Peter could be referring to people who are NOW dead but who had heard the Gospel during their lifetimes (see the rendering of these verses in the *New International Version*).

Or in 3:8 "the spirits" could be "fallen angels" (not departed human beings). Christ would then be declaring His victory over them, not presenting the Gospel to them. And in 4:6 "the dead" could be "the spiritually dead" on the earth who had already heard the Gospel (cp. Eph 2:1,5). The Greek word for "preached" in 3:8 is different from the one in 4:6. The former indicates only an "announcement" -- the latter the proclamation of the Gospel (Edwin A. Blum "1 Peter" in *The Expositor's Bible Commentary*. Ed. Frank E. Gaebelein. Grand Rapids, MI: Zondervan, 1981, pp.241-245).

No (Historic Christianity):

Luke 16:19-31; Heb 9:27:
There is no "second chance" in the hereafter. Judgment occurs at death.

Note: All Scripture references from: *The New King James Version*. Nashville, TN: Thomas Nelson Publishers, 1982, unless otherwise indicated.

The Seventh-Day Sabbath

Scripture Study #16

Note: The position of Seventh-Day Adventists is presented first. Below each Scripture reference is how Seventh-Day Adventists would interpret the verse. After the "BUT" is the reason Darkness to Light ministry disagrees with that interpretation. Then the position of this ministry is given, followed by Scripture verses and interpretations thereof.

Are Christians Required to Keep the Seventh-Day Sabbath?

Yes:

Genesis 2:1-3:
God rested on the Sabbath as an example of what He expects of all peoples for all times.

BUT: There is no record in the Scriptures of anyone keeping the Sabbath before the time of Moses. God made known the Sabbath to Moses on Mount Sinai (Neh 9:13f). The Sabbath was a sign of the Covenant God made with the nation Israel (Exod 31:13-17; Ezek 20:12). But Christians are under the New Covenant (Matt 26:28).

Exodus 20:8-11:
Sabbath observance is one of the Ten Commandments and the reason given for it is the creation order.

BUT: When the Commandments are repeated, the reason given for it is God's deliverance of Israel out of Egypt, not creation (Deut 5:12-15).

Matthew 12:8:
Jesus is "Lord of the Sabbath."

BUT: What does this mean? See verses 1-7, 9-14.

Luke 4:16:
Jesus attended the synagogue on the Sabbath.

BUT: The New Covenant was not yet instituted.

Acts 13:14; 17:1,2:
Paul attended the synagogue on the Sabbath.

BUT: Paul's purpose for attending was to witness to the Jews and Gentiles there (Acts 13:15-44; 17:3f; 18:4).

Colossians 2:16:
Paul uses "Sabbaths" in the plural so he is not referring to the regular seventh-day Sabbath, but to special "sabbaths" during the week.

BUT: The plural "Sabbaths" is used several times in the Gospels to refer to the seventh-day Sabbath, even if it is often (though incorrectly) translated in the singular (e.g. Matt 12:1,5,11,12; Mark 1:21; 2:23,24; 3:2,4; Luke 4:31; 6:2,9, see the ALT for the correct, plural translation).

No:

Exodus 35:1-3; Numbers 15:32-36:
If the Sabbath is still binding, all aspects of the OT Law in regards to it must be obeyed.

Matthew 15:19,20:

"Breaking the Sabbath" is never mentioned in any of the lists of sins in the NT (See also Rom 13:8-10; 1Cor 6:9f; Gal 5:19-25; Col 3:5-9; Rev 21:8).

Mark 10:19:
The command to "Observe the Sabbath" is never repeated in the NT.

Acts 15:10,11:
The Sabbath is part of the OT ceremonial "yoke" Christ has set us free from.

Romans 3:28:
We are "justified by faith apart from the deeds of the law."

Romans 14:5,6:
Christians are free to observe or not observe "days" as one's own conscious permits.

Galatians 5:1-14:
What Paul says in regards to circumcision could easily apply to Sabbath keeping.

Colossians 2:13-17:
Sabbath keeping is simply "a shadow of things to come, but the substance is in Christ."

Hebrews 4:4-16:
The true "rest" for the Christian is salvation in Christ, not Sabbath keeping.

Hebrews 8:1-13:
Sabbath keeping is part of the first covenant that is now "obsolete."

Hebrews 9:1-15:
The tabernacle worship and other OT ceremonial laws were fulfilled in Christ. Thus, these regulations are no longer binding. And Sabbath keeping is linked with the tabernacle and ceremonial laws (Exod 31:1-17; 35:1ff; Lev 23:1ff; 26:2; see also John 4:19-24).

Sunday Worship

Note: Sunday observance is not a "law" that must be obeyed any more than seventh-day Sabbath observance is. But if a day is to be picked for Christians to worship on, the first day of the week is the most logical choice.

Matthew 28:1-9; Mark 16:2-8; Luke 24:1-12; John 20:1-12,19-22:
Jesus rose and revealed Himself on the first day.

Acts 20:7:
Paul had been in Troas seven days; so he could have spoken on the seventh-day, but he chose the first day of the week. And notice the disciples had already gathered together "to break bread" on the first day.

Acts 2:1-4:
The Holy Spirit was given on the first day.

1Corinthians 16:2:
Church collections were to be taken "On the first day of the week...."

Note: All Scripture references from: *The New King James Version.* Nashville, TN: Thomas Nelson Publishers, 1982, unless otherwise indicated.

Questions for Jehovah's Witnesses

Scripture Study #17

Note: After each question, the answer Jehovah's Witnesses (JWs) would give is presented first. Below each Scripture reference is how JWs would interpret the verse. After the "BUT" is the reason Darkness to Light ministry disagrees with their interpretation. Then this ministry's answer is given, followed by Scripture verses and interpretations thereof.

Is it Wrong for a Christian to Receive a Blood Transfusion?

Yes:

Genesis 9:3-5; Leviticus 17:13,14; Acts 15:28,29:
Receiving a blood transfusion is the same as eating blood which is forbidden.

BUT: When someone's well-being was at stake, Jesus freely overturned OT ceremonial laws (Matt 12:1-14). In Acts 15, the recommendation was given simply to prevent any undo stress between Jewish and Gentile Christians (cp. Rom 14:1-17); it was not intended to indicate any OT ceremonial laws are still binding.

137

No:

Matt 15:19,20:
"eating blood" is never included in any of the lists of sins in the NT (See also 1Cor 6:9,10; Gal 5:19-25; Eph 5:3-7; Col 3:5-9; 1Tim 1:8-11; Rev 21:8).

Mark 7:18-23:
What comes out of people is what matters to God, not what goes into them.

Colossians 2:13-17:
Christ fulfilled the "shadows" of OT ceremonial laws and set us free of their requirements!

Acts 10:12-16:
There are no longer any "unclean foods."

Is it Wrong for Christians to Celebrate Birthdays and Holidays?

Yes:

Genesis 40:20; Matthew 14:6:
The Bible records only two birthday celebrations and something bad happened on each one. So God must disprove of them.

BUT: Does the conclusion really follow from the premise? In addition, Pharaoh's birthday was "good" for the butler (Gen 40:21). And even the baker's execution was not "bad" if he was guilty of a capital offense (Gen 9:5f).

No:

Esther 9:18-29:
Holidays and birthdays are celebrated to commemorate important events in the life of a person or society. "Purim" was instituted by the Jews for just such a reason.

Romans 14:4-6; Colossians 2:16,17:
Christians are free to celebrate "days" as one's own conscience permits.

What Does it Mean to Declare the "Name" of God? (Ps 22:22; John 17:26).

Tell people His title is Jehovah:

Exodus 6:1-3:
God instructs Moses to call Him "Jehovah."

BUT: The word "Jehovah" (or better "Yahweh") is from the same root as the term "I Am" (see Exod 3:14). The point of the name is to indicate God's eternal, self-existent nature.

Tell people about the nature of God:

Genesis 2:23; 3:20; 17:5,6; 32:28:
The word "name" in Scripture does not refer to simply a title but indicates something of the character, reputation, or nature of the person (see also Ps 135:13; 138:2; Prov 10:7; Isaiah 7:14; 9:6; 1Cor 1:10,14f).

God has several different "names" in Scripture. Each one is used to indicate a different aspect of His Being: God

Most High (Gen 14:18-22); Almighty God (Gen 17:1f); Jealous (Exod 43:14); Eternal God (Deut 33:27); Living God (Josh 3:10); God of hosts (Isa 1:24); Holy One (Isa 43:3); God of heaven (Jonah 1:9); Heavenly Father (Matt 6:26); King eternal (1Tim 1:17); Only Potentate (1Tim 6:15); Father of lights (James 1:17).

We "praise the name of God" by worshipping Him for possessing these attributes, not by exalting a word (Psalm 48:10; 69:30).

Who are Christians to be Witness of?

Jehovah:

Isaiah 43:10:
Jehovah declares, "You are My witnesses."

BUT: This is the OT and was addressed to Jews, not Christians (see 43:1).

Jesus!

Throughout the NT it is Jesus that Christians are said to be witnesses of.

In the Book of Acts:
1:8; 3:6; 4:10-12,18; 5:28,40-42; 8:5,35; 9:16,20; 11:20,26; 15:26; 16:31; 17:18; 20:21; 21:13; 23:11; 26:28; 28:23,30f.

Elsewhere in the NT:
Mark 9:38-40; Luke 24:47; John 16:13f; 1Cor 2:2; 2Cor 4:5; 5:20; Eph 3:8; Phil 1:15-21; 3:8-10; Col 1:27f; Heb 12:1; 2Pet 3:18; Rev 22:21.

What Should Christians Call God?

Jehovah:

Exodus 6:1-3; Isaiah 43:10,11:
Jehovah is God's proper name.

BUT: This is the OT. Jesus has opened "a new and living way" into the presence of God (Heb 10:20).

Father!
Through faith in Christ, a person can move beyond relating to God on a mere proper-name basis into an intimate, filial relationship with Him! (Heb 4:14-16).

Matt 6:9; Rom 1:7; 1Cor 1:3; 2Cor 1:2; 6:18; Gal 1:4; Eph 1:2; 2:18; Phil 1:2; 4:20; Col 1:2; 1Thes 1:1,3; 3:11,13; 2Thes 1:1f; 2:16; 1Tim 1:2; Phlm 3; Jam 3:9; 1Pet 1:2; 1John 1:2f; 2:13,23f; 3:1; 2John 3f,9; Jude 1.

Those who have trusted in Christ for their salvation can even cry out, "DAD; FATHER!" (Rom 8:15; Gal 4:6; ALT).

Notes:
Additional Scripture Studies with questions relevant to JWs are: *The Person and Life of Jesus Christ*, *The Afterlife*, *Eternity*, and *Christians and the Government*. See also the three studies on the doctrine of the Trinity: *The Doctrine of the Trinity*, *Arguments Against the Trinity*, *More on the Trinity*.

All Scripture references from: The New King James Version. Nashville, TN: Thomas Nelson Publishers, 1982, unless otherwise indicated.

End-Time Prophecy

Scripture Study #18

The Rapture

Note: For the pre-tribulation view, after the Scripture reference is how pre-tribulationists interpret the passage. After the "BUT" is the reason Darkness to Light disagrees with that interpretation. For the post-tribulation view, after the Scripture reference is how post-tribulationists interpret the passage.

Pre-Tribulation

The rapture of the Church will occur before the seven-year "Great Tribulation."

John 14:1-3:
Jesus' promise, "I will come again and receive you to Myself" refers to the pre-trib rapture.

BUT: There is no specific reference as to WHEN this "coming again" is referring to.

1Thessalonians 1:10:
"Jesus, which delivered us from the wrath to come" means Christians won't go through the "Great Tribulation."

BUT: "The wrath to come" refers to the final judgment and eternal punishment in hell, not a mere seven-year period of "tribulation" on the earth (1Thes 5:9,10; Rom 2:5-10; Heb 9:28).

2Thessalonians 2:6-12:

When "He who now restrains will do so until He is taken out of the way" the "Great Tribulation will begin.

BUT: There is no indication of a seven-year "gap" between verses seven and eight. Note verse eight begins with "And then" indicating the events proceeds right after one another. The "unrighteous deception" of verse ten refers not just to Satan's actions during a supposed seven-year period but throughout history.

Revelation 3:10:

Jesus promises to Christians, "I also will keep you from the hour of trial which shall come upon the whole world, to test those who dwell on the earth." So Christians will not go through the Great Tribulation.

BUT: According to the pre-millennial/ dispensational general method of interpreting the Revelation (see below), chapter three is during the period of "the things which are" (i.e. occurring during John's lifetime). So Jesus' promise in 3:10, by the dispensationalist's own division of the book, cannot be referring to end-time events. Those prophecies do not begin until the next chapter. The promise is specific to the church of Philadelphia at that time.

But even if the promise were referring to end-time events, it would still not be referring to a pre-trib rapture. The only other place in Scripture where the phrase "keep ... from" occurs is in John 17:15. Only there Jesus says, "I do not pray that You should take them out of the world, but that You should keep them from the evil one." So to be "kept from" does not mean to be taken out of the world but to be "kept" by God in the sense of experiencing His comfort while undergoing worldly tribulations.

Revelation 4:1:

When Jesus says to John, "Come up here," it is symbolic of the Church being called up to heaven before the tribulation.

BUT: There is no indication in the text whatsoever that John is symbolic of the Church.

Revelation 7:1-8:

The sealing of "the servants of our God" so they would not be harmed is symbolic of the Church being taken out of the world before the tribulation.

BUT: The text specifically says those who are sealed are 144,000 Jews. But even if this is taken symbolically of the Church as a whole, the text still says nothing about them being taken out of the world. They are being kept from harm while still on the earth.

Post-Tribulation

The rapture is concurrent with the Second Coming.

Matthew 25:1,6-10:

The coming of the Bridegroom is concurrent with the "wise virgins" being taken away.

1 Thessalonians 4:16-17:

The Coming of Christ is concurrent with believers being "caught up" to be with Him.

Titus 2:13:

It is the "glorious appearing of our great God and Savior Jesus Christ" that is the "blessed hope" of believers--not the rapture.

Hebrews 9:28:
Believers are eagerly waiting for Christ to "appear a second time" not for the rapture.

The Millennium

Note: Darkness to Light does not take a position as to which millennial view is correct. So for each view, the Scriptures quoted to support each view are given, along with the supporters' interpretation thereof, without comment.

Pre-millennial

Christ will return and reign on this earth for 1000 years. The righteous will be raised before the millennium, the wicked afterwards. The promises to the nation Israel will be literally fulfilled at this time. The creation of the new heavens and new earth will occur after this 1000-year period.

Genesis 8:22:
God promises "day and night" will not cease while the earth remains. The promises to David must be fulfilled while this covenant is still in force (Gen 22:17; Jer 33:20,25). It is only after the creation of the "new heavens and the new earth" that night ceases (Rev 22:5).

Psalm 2:7-9:
Christ receives "the nations as His inherence" during the millennium.

Psalm 37:9-11:

"those who wait on the LORD, They shall inherit the earth." This will happen during the millennium (see also Matt 5:5).

Psalm 46:8-10:

"wars cease to the end of the earth" during the millennium.

Psalm 102:12-17:

The LORD will "build up Zion" and "appear in His glory" during the millennium.

Isaiah 2:1-4; Micah 4:1-3:

Descriptions of the millennium.

A-millennial

No literal 1000-year millennium. The Second Coming is concurrent with the creation of the new heavens and the new earth. The Second Coming and the final judgment of both the righteous and the wicked are concurrent. The "millennium" is simply the Church Age.

Isaiah 11:1-16; 65:17-25:

The supposed "millennial" earth and the eternal earth are described in the same way.

Psalm 50:10; 105:8; Daniel 7:10,11; Revelation 5:11:

The word "thousand" in Scripture often indicates a large but indeterminate number. So it is not necessary to take it literally in Revelation 20:4-6.

Daniel 12:2; Matthew 25:46; John 5:29; Acts 24:15:

The resurrections of the just and the unjust occur together. There is no thousand-year period separating them.

Note: Pre-millennialists will quote Isaiah 61:1,2 to try to show it is possible for prophecy to "skip" a long period of time in-between two events which are described as one. The idea is, Isaiah 61:1 and the first phrase of verse two refer to the First Coming. But "the day of vengeance of our God" then means Isaiah is looking forward to the Second Coming. So two events described as one are actually separated by the entire Church Age.

However, the next phrase is "To comfort all who mourn." God comforts us now, in this age (2Cor 1:4; 1Peter 5:7). The "day of vengeance" occurs when someone dies (Heb 9:27). It is not a reference to the final judgment. So Isaiah 61:1,2 can be interpreted without inserting any "gap" between the phrases. So it cannot be used to support the "gap" theory in other verses.

Matthew 24:36-44; 1Thessalonians 5:2; 2Peter 3:10; Revelation 16:15:
The Second Coming and the end of time are both described as Jesus coming "as a thief."

Matthew 25:31-46:
The Second Coming and final judgment are concurrent (compare Titus 2:13).

Hebrews 1:10-12:
The heavens continue to decay until the Lord "changes" them; there is no 1000-year hiatus.

Post-millennial

Christ will return after the preaching of the Gospel has ushered in a 1000-year reign of righteousness on the earth. Note: Some of these Scriptures could also support an a-millennial position

Psalm 22:27:
The LORD "rules over the nations" now, so a future "millennial" reign is not necessary. Also, since God does now reign, the Gospel can change the earth now, before the Second Coming.

Psalm 24:1:
"The earth is the LORD's" now; again, a future "millennial" reign is not necessary (see also Psalm 47:2; 97:5; 103:19; Daniel 2:31-45).

Daniel 7:13,14; Acts 2:26:
Jesus is now reigning. He does need to wait for a future millennium to do so, and His Gospel can change the world.

Matthew 12:28:
The kingdom of God has already come. Satan has already been defeated.

Matthew 13:31-50:
The kingdom of God is to grow and become a reality before the Second Coming (see also Mark 4:26-29).

Matthew 16:18:
Christ declares, "the gates of Hades shall not prevail against" His Church. And note, "gates" are defensive, not offensive weapons. So Christ is not merely promising that Satan will not triumph over the Church but that the Church

will triumph over Satan. It can do so now through the preaching of the Gospel.

Matthew 28:18-20:

Believers are commanded to "make disciples of all the nations." We are not to wait for Christ to return for all nations to be Christianized.

Luke 17:20,21:

The kingdom of God is already here as it changes each person from within.

John 12:31,32:

Satan has already been "cast out." So the Gospel can succeed in changing the world.

1Corinthians 15:24-48:

Christ is now reigning as His enemies are being put under His feet through the preaching of the Gospel.

Ephesians 2:19-22:

The Church is now growing so that it will fill the earth.

Colossians 1:13:

Satan has no authority over believers. So they can preach the Gospel unhindered.

Method of Interpreting the Revelation

Note: Below is a description of the general method of how supporters of each of the above three views interpret the Revelation, along with their interpretation of important passages in the Revelation.

Pre-millennial

Revelation 1:19:
"the things which you have seen" are recorded in chapter 1; "the things which are" are seen in chapters 2 and 3; "the things which will take place after this" are in chapters 4-22 and describe events that will occur during the end-times.

Revelation 19:11-20:15:
All events interpreted "literally."

Revelation 21:1:
There is no "sea" on the eternal earth but there is on the millennial earth (compare Psalm 72:8, "sea" is the same word in the Septuagint).

A-millennial

"Progressive parallelism"
The Revelation goes through progressive cycles, each paralleling the previous one (describing similar circumstances). Each repeated cycle begins at the time of John but extends further into the future. Chapter grouping of cycles: 1-3; 4-7; 8-11; 12-14; 15-16; 17-19; 20-22.

Revelation 20:1-3:
The binding of Satan is a reference to his defeat at the cross and the Christian's authority over demonic powers (compare Matt 12:28,29; Mark 3:27; Luke 10:17-19; John 12:31; 16:11; Col 2:15).

Revelation 20:4:
"Souls" are raised at the beginning of the "millennium"-- not bodies. So this is a reference to sinners being

regenerated during the Church Age, not the physical resurrection of believers prior to some millennium (compare Eph 2:1-6).

Revelation 21:1:
"no more sea" means there are no wicked (compare Isaiah 57:20; **BUT:** The Greek of the Septuagint is different).

Post-millennial

Revelation 1:1:
John is being shown things which will "shortly take place." Chapters 1-3 refer to events currently occurring. Chapters 4-11 describe the Jewish persecutions of the Church in the first century. Chapters 12-18 describe the Roman persecutions of the first to fourth centuries. Only chapters 19-22 discuss history's final scenes.

Revelation 19:1-16:
A reference to the preaching of "The Word of God" overcoming the earth (verse 13; Note: the phrase "The Word of God" is never used to describe Christ elsewhere in Scripture). So this chapter is not describing the Second Coming.

Arguments Against Dispensationalism

Along with the above arguments against pre-tribulationalism, following are some arguments against other tenants of dispensationalism. Note also, not all pre-millennialists are dispensationalists. The "historic pre-millennial" position agrees with dispensationalism in regards to the millennium following Christ's return. But the former disagrees with the latter on other points, such as the timing of the rapture. Historic pre-millennialism is post-trib, but dispensationalism is pre-trib.

1) **The land promise is already fulfilled:** Gen 13:14; Josh 21:43-45; 1Kings 4:12; Neh 9:7,8.

2) **The Church is "Spiritual Israel" (There is only one people of God, not two):**

Old Testament passages referring to Israel are applied to the Church in the New Testament:
Exod 19:6; Deut 7:6; 1Pet 2:9/ Ps 22:22,23; Heb 2:10-12/ Isa 54:4; Jer 3:13; Hos 2:19,20; 2Cor 1:1; 11:2; Rev 19:6-9; 21:9/ Jer 31:31-34; Luke 22:20; 2Cor 3:2-6; Heb 10:14-18; 12:22-24/ Hos 2:23; Rom 9:24-26; 2Pet 2:10/ Joel 2:28-32; Acts 2:16-21,39; 10:44-48/ Amos 9:11f; Acts 15:14-17.

New Testament references showing the Church is true Israel:
Matt 8:11; John 10:16; Acts 7:38; Rom 4:9-18; 1Cor 12:13; Gal 3:7-29; Eph 2:11-22; Col 2:11-14; Heb 2:9-18; 3:3-6; 8:1-13; 11:39,40; Jam 1:1; 2:2; 5:14; Rev 21:12-14.

Descriptions of a True Israelite: Luke 19:9; John 1:47; 3:1-10; 8:31-47; Rom 2:28,29; 9:6-8; Gal 3:7-9,29; Phil 3:3.

3) **Old Testament prophecies and types are not always fulfilled literally in the New Testament:**

97 prophecies are mentioned in the New Testament as being fulfilled in Christ. Five different methods are utilized (with examples):

1) Literal (used only 34 times out of the 97 prophecy fulfillments): Micah 5:2; Matt 2:3-6.
2) Typological: Hos 11:1; Matt 2:14,15/ Mal 4:5,6; 17:12.
3) Analogical: Jer 31:15; Matt 2:16-18.
4) General sense: Judg 13:5; Ps 22:6; Isa 11:1; 53:3; Matt 2:23.
5) Verses referring to Yahweh applied to Jesus: Ps 102:25-27; Heb 1:10,11/ Mal 3:11; Mark 1:2.

Note: All Scripture references from: *The New King James Version.* Nashville, TN: Thomas Nelson Publishers, 1982, unless otherwise indicated.

End-Time Prophecy: Scripture Study. Contained in the book *Scripture Workbook.* Copyright © 1999-2000 by Gary F. Zeolla of Darkness to Light ministry - http://www.dtl.org

Ethics

"But solid food belongs to those who are of full age, that is, those who by reason of use have their senses exercised to discern both good and evil" (Heb 5:14).

Divorce and Remarriage

Scripture Study #19

Verses to Consider

In the OT: Gen 2:23f; Lev 21:1,7,13f; Deut 24:1-4; Ezek 44:21f; Ezra 9:1-10:44; Jer 3:1,8; Mal 2:13-16.

In the NT: Matt 5:31f; 19:3-12; Mark 10:2-12; Luke 16:18; Rom 7:2f; 1Cor 7:10-16,39f; 1Tim 3:2,12.

Comments

Genesis 2:23,24:
The "oneness" between a husband and wife reflects the unity in plurality of the Godhead (cp. Gen 1:26f; Deut 6:4).

Leviticus 21:1,7,13,14; Ezekiel 44:21,22:
OT priests had to marry virgins. In the NT, all believers are priests (1Pet 1:1f; 2:9; Rev 5:9f). However, the NT allows the marriage of widows (Rom 7:3).

Deuteronomy 24:1-4:
"Some uncleanness" cannot be adultery since this would require execution (22:22). However, it does refer to something "shameful" or "disgraceful" (cp. use in 1Sam 20:30; Isa 20:4). The purpose of the passage was to put a check on frivolous divorces, to prevent women from being treated like property, and to strengthen the marriage covenant (v.5). Also note, the woman is "defiled" as a

result of remarrying after being divorced (v.4 and see Jer 3:1,8).

Ezra 9:1-10:44:
Ezra commands the divorce of men who had married pagan wives. However, "One should not develop a contemporary approach to marriage or divorce from this extraordinary incident, since God gives clear and explicit instructions elsewhere regarding marriage and divorce" (Criswell, p.647).

Also, when Nehemiah was faced with the same problem, he did not require divorce. But he did explain the dangers of inter-faith marriages and commanded the guilty not to allow their children to follow in their footsteps (Neh 13:23-27; see also 1Cor 7:12f).

Malachi 2:13-16:
God "hates divorce" because it is a breaking of a covenant between God, the man, and his wife. A man should learn to "rejoice with the wife of your youth" (see Prov 5:15-23).

Matthew 5:31,32:
Jesus reinforces ideas found in the OT. Divorce is not to be taken lightly. The only justifiable reason for a man to divorce his wife is if she has committed "fornication" against him. This word refers to having sex with anyone other than one's spouse (Criswell, p.1343). Except in the case of fornication, if a man divorces his wife he "causes her to commit adultery" since she will probably remarry. The man who marries her also commits adultery.

Matthew 19:3-12:
Jesus reaffirms that Gen 1:27; 2:24 means marriage is to be for a lifetime. Divorce only happens "because of the hardness of your hearts." Also, to Matt 5:31f, He adds that the man divorcing his wife and remarrying is committing

adultery (again, except if the divorce occurred due to fornication). Also, "not to marry" (v.10) refers to living a life of celibacy. Pre-marital sex is, of course, a sin in itself (1Thes 4:3-8).

Mark 10:2-12:

In addition to the above, here Jesus adds that for a woman to divorce her husband and to marry another is also adultery (v.12).

Romans 7:2,3; 1Cor 7:39:

Paul repeats the idea it is adultery to remarry. However, if the spouse has died the person is "free" to remarry.

1Corinthians 7:10-16:

Paul reaffirms that marriage partners should not separate. However, if a separation does occur, he gives two options: either lifetime celibacy or reconciliation of the marriage. Remarriage is not given as an option for Christians. But, if the divorce resulted due to an unbeliever leaving a believer, then the believer "is not under bondage." This phrase probably refers to the right to remarry.

Thus, Paul adds abandonment to fornication as a justifiable reason for getting a divorce. However, it must be noted, the believer does not have the option of leaving the unbeliever. This would also imply that if both partners are Christians, neither has the right to leave the marriage.

1Timothy 3:2,12:

The phrase "husband of one wife" could refer to not being divorced and then remarried, but it more likely forbids a polygamist from being an elder or deacon.

Physical Abuse:

What about physical abuse? Does the woman have a right to a divorce if her husband is physically abusing her? The Bible never specifically addresses this topic. However, a few comments are in order on this difficult subject.

Paul commands, "Wives, submit to your own husbands" (Eph 5:22). This cannot be taken to mean a woman should tolerate physical abuse. The same passage commands husbands "love your wives" (v.25). A man who is abusing his wife is not following this command.

If a woman is in an abusive situation, she should most definitely get herself out of the place of danger. Personally, I would consider physical abuse a justifiable reason for divorce, and I am sure many would agree with this assessment.

Conclusion

The Bible is clear--marriage is for a lifetime. To marry, get a divorced, and then to remarry is adultery. This is always true unless the divorce occurred due to adultery or abandonment (and possibly physical abuse). These restrictions may seem harsh, but think of the beneficial consequences if people were to accept these standards.

Accepting that only one marriage is permissible would make people much more cautious about who they marry. Marriage would no longer be entered into in the flippant way it often is today.

Knowing that to get a divorce would mean a lifetime of celibacy would be an encouragement to couples to put as much effort as possible into their marriage. Struggling through problems, rather than just giving up, can lead to a deeper and more meaningful relationship between a husband and wife. God blesses when people abide by His standards of behavior (Ps 1:1-3; 119:1f; Prov 8:32-36; 29:18).

And finally, for anyone who is already guilty of any the sins mentioned above, forgiveness and a fresh start is available to you if you repent and trust in Jesus Christ for the forgiveness of your sins (Ps 51:1-17; Matt 1:21; 26:28; Rom 4:1-8; 7:24-8:1; 13:12-14; 2Cor 5:17; Titus 3:3-8).

Bibliography:

All Scripture references from: *The New King James Version*. Nashville, TN: Thomas Nelson Publishers, 1982, unless otherwise indicated.

Criswell, W.A. ed. *The Believer's Study Bible: New King James Version*. Nashville: Thomas Nelson, 1991.

Divorce and Remarriage: Scripture Study. Contained in the book *Scripture Workbook*. Copyright © 1999-2000 by Gary F. Zeolla of Darkness to Light ministry - http://www.dtl.org

Capital Punishment

For Pre-meditated Murder

Scripture Study #20

Pro Arguments

I.   Link between sin and death instituted by God (Gen 2:15-17).

II. Noahic Covenant.

    A.   Made with all people (Gen 9:9,12).
    B.   Continues until "the new heaven and new earth" (Gen 8:22; Rev 22:5).
    C.   Commands execution of murderers (Gen 9:5f).
    D.   Reason given for Capital Punishment (CP) for murder is the sanctity of human life.
    E.   Precedes Mosaic Covenant by at least 1000 years.

III. Mosaic Covenant.

    A.   Mosaic Covenant only with the Hebrews (Exod 2:24f).
    B.   Includes 18 Capital offenses including murder (Exod 21:12; Lev 24:17f,21).
    C.   But execution for murder is distinct from the other 17.
        1.   It is also part of the Noahic Covenant.
        2.   Only offense with reason given for it the image of God in humans (Gen 9:6).
        3.   No possibility of reconciliation or restitution (Matt 5:23f; Luke 19:8).

IV. Principles of Mosaic Covenant for dealing with alleged murderers.

    A. Due process before judgment (Numb 35:12).
    B. Need two or three witness for conviction and false witness to be punished (Deut 19:15-19).
    C. No ransom allowed, only execution (Numb 35:32).
    D. Only for pre-meditated murder, not unintentional or spontaneous killing (Numb 35:22-28; Dt 4:41-42; 19:4-12).
    E. Reasons given for executing convicted murderers.
        1. "that it may go well with you" (Deut 19:13).
        2. So the land will not be defiled (Numb 35:33f).
        3. Deterrence (Deut 13:10f; 17:12f; 19:20).

V. New Testament times.

    A. CP has been in place for at least 2400 years for all peoples.
    B. Specific CP laws in effect for Israel for 1400 years.
    C. Roman and Jewish cultures accept and practice CP (Luke 23:39-41; Acts 25:11).

VI. Jesus.

    A. Never explicitly overturns CP law.
    B. Upholds authority of OT (Matt 5:17-19).
    C. Declares Pilate's authority to execute is God-given (John 19:11f).
    D. Never mentions any alternate form of punishment for murderers.
    E. Did not release either of the criminals crucified with Him from their crosses (Luke 23:39-43).

VII. Paul.

    A. Upholds God-given authority of the state (Rom 13:1f cp. Isa 44:28; Dan 4:17).
    B. Teaches individuals do not have authority to execute God's wrath (Rom 12:19-21).
    C. But, declares the authority of the state to execute the wrath of God (Rom 13:4).
    D. Declared punishment includes the use of the sword (Greek, *machaira*).
        1. Used by the government to execute (Matt 26:51f; Acts 12:1f).
        2. Always viewed as instrument of death (Acts 16:27; Rev 6:4; 13:3,10,14).
    E. Reason for government: so society is at peace (1Tim 2:1f).
    F. Never mentions any alternate form of punishment for murderers.
    G. Recognizes legitimacy of CP (Acts 25:11).

VIII.   Peter.

    A. Upholds authority of the state and its right to punish wrongdoers (1Pet 2:13f).
    B. Never mentions any alternate form of punishment for murderers.

Con Arguments and Rebuttals

Note: Below the Scripture reference is the interpretation for the verse by those who believe the Bible teaches capital punishment should not be practiced. After the "BUT" is the rebuttal to this interpretation.

Genesis 1:26-28:
People are created in the image of God, so murderers should not be executed.

BUT: God says the exact opposite! It is because of the *Imago Dei* murderers must be executed (Gen 9:6).

Genesis 4:9-12:
God doesn't have Cain executed for murdering Abel.

BUT:
A. Time is before authority given to state to execute (Genesis chapter 4 vs. chapter 9).
B. Wandering, not life imprisonment is the declared punishment (Gen 4:12).
C. Killing of murderers assumed to be the norm even then (Gen 4:14).
D. Violence of pre-flood world brought on its destruction (Gen 6:11).
 1. Wide-spread violence may have resulted from no state authority to execute (Deut 13:10f; 17:12f; 19:20).
 2. CP authority given immediately after flood and before re-civilization of the earth.
 3. God has right to pardon; we are to obey His commands (Rom 9:15; Josh 1:17).

Genesis 9:6:
A prediction of what will happen; not a commandment of what to do.

BUT:
A. Imperfect, jussive form of verb used here is also used in the 10 Commandments.
B. Elsewhere in Gen 9 are promises and commands, not predictions.
C. Verse 6 is explanation of how God will require the lifeblood as mentioned in v.5.

Deuteronomy 19:1-6:

Murderers not executed but allowed to flee to a city of refuge.

BUT: Cities of refuge for unintentional killings, not for pre-meditated murder (see vv.4,11-13).

Matthew 5:38-44:

Vengeance prohibited for Christians, mercy and love instead.

BUT:
A. In the Sermon on the Mount, Jesus is discussing personal not state actions (Matt 5:1).
B. God reserves the right to Himself to execute vengeance (Rom 12:19).
C. One way He carries out His vengeance is through the state (Rom 13:4).
D. A "slap on the cheek" is a verbal insult, not a life-threatening assault (v.39).

John 8:2-11:

The woman caught in adultery is prevented from being executed by Jesus.

BUT:
A. Textual difficulty of this passage makes it a precarious proof text.
B. Adultery, not murder, is the crime.
   1. The argument here is for execution of those convicted of pre-meditated murder.
   2. Remember difference between Noahic and Mosaic covenants.
C. Witnesses have all left; at least two are needed for a conviction (v.9 and Deut 19:15).
D. Jews at this time did not have authority to execute (John 18:31).

Romans 12:17-21; 13:8-10:

Forgiveness and love, not vengeance, should be shown to others.

BUT:
A. Prohibits personal vendettas and taking the law into one's own hands.
B. Rom 13:1-7 is included in-between these passages to prevent misunderstanding them as referring to prohibitions on God-ordained, governmental actions.

Ephesians 2:14-16; Gal 3:13:

Jesus paid for sin, so murderers should not be executed.

BUT:
A. Forgiven as far as eternal salvation goes but still reap what we sow in this life (Gal 6:7).
B. If murderers should not be executed, what should be done with them?
   1. No Scriptural support for life imprisonment or any other form of punishment.
   2. If just forgiven without punishment:
      a. All other criminals would also have to be released.
      b. Anarchy would result (see again Gen 6:11; 1Tim 2:1f).
C. Despite forgiveness in Christ, death can still result from sin (Acts 5:1-11; Rom 5:12).

Conclusion

Two main issues must be remembered:

A. The difference between the Noahic vs. the Mosaic Covenants.
B. The difference between personal vengeances vs. God-ordained governmental actions.

Capital Punishment: Scripture Study. Contained in the book *Scripture Workbook.* Copyright © 1999-2000 by Gary F. Zeolla of Darkness to Light ministry - http://www.dtl.org

Christians and the Government

Scripture Study #21

Note:
After each question, the answer which Darkness to Light ministry disagrees with is given first. Below each Scripture reference is how "the other side" interprets the verse. After the "BUT" is the reason this ministry disagrees with that interpretation. Then the answer this ministry would give to the question is given, followed by Scripture verses and interpretations thereof.

Is it Wrong for Christians to be Involved in the Secular Government?

Yes (Jehovah's Witnesses, Mennonites, and other Anabaptist groups):

Luke 12:13,14:
Jesus refused to become involved in governmental matters.

BUT: The case needed to be taken to the proper, God-ordained authorities (Rom 13:1). Jesus was not in this position at this time.

Mark 12:17:
Believers are to render things to God not "Caesar."

BUT: The verse teaches believers are to be involved in BOTH secular and spiritual matters.

John 17:16:

Believers are not to be "of the world."

BUT: What does "the world" mean? In this context, it refers to those who are opposed to God and who try to institute systems contrary to His ways (1John 5:19). Believers are called to be "salt" and "light" to these people and to transform society according to godly principles (Matt 5:13-15). We are promised that our faith is able to "overcome the world" (1John 5:4f).

Acts 5:29:

Believers "ought to obey God rather than men."

BUT: We are to obey the government at all times unless it requires something ungodly (Rom 13:2; Dan 6:7-10).

No:

Genesis 9:6,7:

The institution of the death penalty was given to, and to be carried out by, all peoples (9:9). And execution is a function of the secular government (Rom 13:4).

Genesis 41:3-43; 45:5-8; Acts 7:9,10:

Joseph was placed in the Egyptian government and used mightily by God in his governmental office.

Nehemiah 2:1-10:

Nehemiah was an official in the court of King Artaxerxes of Persia and used by God in that capacity.

Esther 4:13,14; 10:3:

God placed Esther in the court of King Ahasuerus of Persia to work out His purposes. Mordecai was later also in the Persian government.

Daniel 1:1-3:

Daniel, Shadrach, Meshach, and Abed-Nego were used by God in the Babylonian government.

Luke 1:3:

Theophilus was most likely a Christian. Luke addresses him with the title "most excellent" which was generally used for governmental officials.

Romans 13:1

Secular government was instituted by God.

Romans 16:23:

Paul's companion Eratus was "the treasurer of the city"--a government position.

Is it Wrong for Christians to be Involved in the Military?

Yes: (Jehovah's Witnesses, Mennonites, and other Anabaptist groups):

Matthew 5:38-42:

We are told to "turn the other cheek."

BUT: This passage refers to personal, not governmental actions. And at this time the Jews were not to resist the Roman Empire since they could not win (Luke 21:20-24). Also a "slap on the cheek" is not a physical attack but simply an insult.

Matthew 26:51,52:

Jesus tells Peter not to fight back.

BUT: The situation is not one of war but of an arrest being made by the proper authorities for such an action (cp. Luke 22:52; John 18:31).

2Corinthians 10:3,4:
We are to fight with spiritual not carnal weapons.

BUT: The passage refers to the spreading of the Gospel, not national defense.

Isaiah 2:2-4:
"They shall beat their swords into plowshares, and their spears into pruning hooks."

BUT: This is a description of a future age. For this age, we are told to do the exact opposite (Joel 3:10).

No:

Genesis 14:14-16:
Abraham uses military force to free his nephew and others taken captive.

Exodus 15:3:
"The LORD is a man of war; the LORD is His name."

Leviticus 26:3,7:
Obedience to God leads to success in battle.

Deuteronomy 20:1:
God fights for His people.

Judges 3:1,2:
God providentially arranges history so that each generation "be taught to know war."

Judges 3:10:
The Spirit leads Othniel "out to war."

Judges 4:21; 5:24-27:
Jael is praised for bringing about a military victory.

Judges 19:1-20:48:
When the people in one tribe of God's people sinned, the other tribes go to battle against them. In 20:27,28 God is asked, and He specifically commands the Israelites to go into battle against their brothers.

1Samuel 15:3,7-9,19-26:
God instructs Saul to go to war against Amalek. God rejects Saul as being king when he does not follow God's specific commands about how to conduct the war.

2Samuel 22:35:
David praises God because "He teaches my hands to make war..." (see also Ps 18:34; 144:1).

Psalm 18:31-42:
David praises God for victory in battle.

Proverbs 20:18:
"by wise counsel wage war."

Ecclesiastes 3:8:
There is "A time of war."

Jeremiah 48:10:
When God pronounces judgment, "cursed is he who keeps back his sword from blood."

Joel 3:10:
In this age, nations are told to, "Beat your plowshares into swords and your pruning hooks into spears."

Matthew 8:5-13:

Jesus does not rebuke the centurion for being part of the Roman military. Instead, Jesus commends him for his great faith and answers his request for the healing of his servant.

Luke 3:14:

When the soldiers ask John the Baptist what they should do, he does not tell them to cease to be soldiers. Instead, John tells them to carry out their duties in an appropriate manner.

Luke 14:28-32:

Jesus uses an analogy from war alongside other analogies without a hint that the act of war is wrong in itself.

Acts 10:1,2,34,35:

Cornelius the centurion is said to be a man who "fears [God] and works righteousness."

Romans 13:1-4:

Government is instituted by God. A part of its function is the use of deadly force ("the sword") against "him who practices evil." Note: "the sword" (Greek, *machaira*) is always viewed in Scripture as an instrument of death (Acts 16:27; Rev 6:4; 13:3,10,14). It is used by the government to execute (Matt 26:51f; Acts 12:1f). So this passage would apply to the use of deadly force in times of war and in the execution of criminals. For the latter, see the Study *Capital Punishment* .

Notes:

The above Scripture Study should NOT be construed as meaning that this ministry advocates any kind of church-state system. The questions are simply about whether Christians can vote, hold public office, and be involved in other political and governmental activities.

Darkness to Light believes in freedom of religion as guaranteed in the First Amendment to The Constitution of the United States, "Congress shall make no law respecting an establishment of religion, or prohibiting the free exercise thereof" (Matt 22:21; John 18:36).

All Scripture references from: *The New King James Version*. Nashville, TN: Thomas Nelson Publishers, 1982, unless otherwise indicated.

Miscellaneous Subjects

Scripture Study #22

Sexual Issues

1) Marrying unbelievers:
Gen 6:1-5; 34:12-17; Deut 6:6-9; 7:1-4; Num 25:1-3; Josh 23:11-13; Judg 3:5-8; 13:4-21; 1Kings 11:1-4; Ezra 10:1-19; Neh 13:23-27; 1Cor 7:39; 2Cor 6:14f.

2) Singles and sex:
Gen 2:24; 34:7; 39:7-12; Deut 22:13-30; 2Sam 13:1-17; Prov 5:15-20; Song 8:4,8-10; Matt 5:27-30; Rom 13:10-14; 14:21; 1Cor 6:15-20; 7:1-9,25-28; 13:4-8; 1Thes 4:1-8; 1Tim 4:12; 5:1f (cp. Lev 18:6-9); 2Tim 2:22; Heb 13:4f.

3) Abortion:
Exod 21:22f; Judg 13:5-7; 2Sam 11:1-27; Ps 22:10; 82:3f; 106:35-39; 139:13-16; Prov 6:16f; 31:2; Isa 44:24; 45:10; 49:1,5,15; Jer 1:5; 2:34; Hos 9:15f; Amos 1:13; Matt 1:18f; Luke 1:5,39-44; Acts 3:2; Gal 1:15.   The real reason abortionists defend their practice: Acts 19:23-27.

4) Homosexuality:
Gen 2:24; 19:4f,24 (cp. Ezek 16:49f); Lev 18:22; 20:13; Rom 1:24-27; 1Cor 6:9f; 1Tim 1:10.

An Important Question for Some Men

Is it wrong for men to wear beards?

Yes:

1Corinthians 11:4-7:
Women are not to shave but men are.

BUT: The passage never actually says men have to shave. Moreover, beards are not even being discussed; "shaved" cannot be referring to the removal of facial hair since women do not shave their faces! (11:6f). The passage is talking about hair on the top of the head, not on the face (11:14f). Being "shaved" refers to being BALD (cp. Acts 21:24).

No:

Leviticus 19:27; 21:5:
Israelites were forbidden to trim their beards in accordance with pagan rituals. This command obviously assumes men will be wearing beards.

2Samuel 10:4,5:
David's servants are captured and disgraced by having half of their beards shaved off. David orders them to wait till their beards have grown back before retuning.

Isaiah 7:20:
Being forcibly shaved is a sign of being under God's judgement.

Isaiah 15:2; Jeremiah 48:37:
Beards were shaved during times of deep mourning. Implies men have beards under normal circumstances.

Men in the Bible with beards: Joseph (Gen 41:14), Aaron (Ps 133:2), Ezekiel (Ezek 5:1), Ezra (Ezra 9:3), and

Jesus! (Isa 50:6, a prophecy about the Messiah, cp. Isa 52:14; Matt 26:67; 27:27-31).

Final Note: The word "beard" does not appear in the NT. Most notably, Paul does not bring up the subject of beards, or the lack thereof, when listing the qualifications for Christian ministers (1Tim 3:1-13; Titus 1:5-9; cp. 1Sam 16:7).

A Couple of Serious Questions

1) Are all people dying in infancy saved?

Yes:

2Samuel 12:22,23:
David is confident he will "go to" his departed infant.

Matthew 18:14:
"it is not the will of your Father who is in heaven that one of these little ones should perish." So all infants who die are saved.

BUT: But at the beginning of this section, Jesus specifically refers to "these little ones who believe in Me" (18:6). So the "little ones" who will not perish are not infants, but are old enough to be believers in Christ. So this passage tells us nothing about the fate of dying infants or of dying unbelieving children. It does, however, support the doctrine of eternal security.

No:

Genesis 6:5:
All the people in the antediluvian world, except for Noah and his family, were considered wicked and

destroyed in the Flood. This would have included children and infants.

Genesis 18:16-33:
Abraham plead with God that if ten righteous are found in Sodom and Gomorrah that the cities would not be destroyed (v.32). Surely, these two large cities had at least ten infants in them, but they were destroyed anyway.

1Samuel 15:3:
The LORD, through Samuel, tells King Saul "to both kill man and woman, infant and nursing child" among the unrighteous Amalekites.

Psalm 137:9:
The "little ones" of Babylon are to be "dashed against the rocks."

Ezekiel 9:1-11:
The "men with fine linen (probably angels) are told by the LORD to "Utterly slay old and young men, maidens and little children and women" in sinful Jerusalem.

Conclusion:
"Elect infants, dying in infancy, are regenerated and saved by Christ through the Spirit, who worketh when, and where, and how He pleaseth. So also are all other elect persons, who are incapable of being outwardly called by the ministry of the word" (*Westminster Confession*; Chapter X: III).

2) What about those who never heard the Gospel?

A. **"all have sinned"** - Rom 3:23; People are under the wrath of God because of their sins, not just unbelief: John 3:36; Rev 21:8.

B. General revelation: Ps 19:1-6; Eccl 3:11; Rom 1:18-23.

C. Degrees of punishment: Matt 11:20-24; Luke 12:47; John 19:10; Heb 10:29.

D. Narrow way: Exod 20:1-5; Isa 43:10-13; Matt 7:13f; 11:27; Luke 13:22-30; John 3:36; 5:23; 10:9; 14:6; Acts 4:12; Eph 2:11f; 1Tim 2:5; 1John 5:12.

E. Non-Judeo/ Christian religions: 1Ki 19:17f; 1Chr 16:26; Ps 96:5; Jer 2:11; 5:7; 10:8-11; 16:19-21: Hab 2:18-20; John 10:7-10; Acts 14:11-15; 17:16,22-31; 19:26; 26:17f; Rom 1:18-23; 1Cor 1:18-21; 8:4; 10:19-22; Gal 1:8; Col 2:8; 1Thes 1:9f.

F. No second chance: Luke 16:19-31; 2Cor 6:1f; Heb 3:15-4:11; 9:27f; Rev 9:20f; 16:9.

Word Faith Movement

1) Health and wealth "gospel" not Biblical:
Job 2:7; Ps 34:19; 37:16; Hab 3:17-19; Prov 30:8f; Matt 3:4; 6:11,19-34; 8:20; Mark 10:17-23; Luke 12:15-21; 16:19-31; Acts 14:22; 16:33; Rom 8:18-39; 1Cor 4:8-13; 2Cor 1:9; 4:8-10,16-18; 11:22-30; 12:7-10; Gal 4:13; Phil 2:25-27; 4:12; Col 4:14; 1Tim 5:23; 6:5-11; 2Tim 4:20; Heb 11:24-26,36-40.

2) Negative confessions:
Ruth 1:20f; Ps 6:2f,6f; 10:1; 13:1f; 22:1f; 25:16-18; 31:9-13; 32:3-5; 33:6-9; 38:1-22; 41:17; 42:9-11; 43:2; 55:4; 70:5; 88:1-18; 142:2; Dan 3:17f; Matt 26:38; Mark 9:24.

3) Alternate views:

Deut 28:1-14; Josh 1:8:
Prosperity follows obedience.

BUT: These passages are talking about national not individual fortunes.

2Chron 16:12:
Asa condemned for seeking the physicians rather than the Lord.

BUT: Doesn't say anything about seeking the Lord AND the physicians. Also, doctors at this time were very ineffective and often used pagan practices.

Isa 53:5; Matt 8:16f:
Healing is in the Atonement.

BUT: Matt 8:16f is before the death of Jesus, so it is irrelevant. Further, the "healing" Jesus attained for us at the cross was spiritual (1Pet 2:24).

Various Subjects

1) God as feminine:
Ruth 2:9; Ps 22:9f; 123:2; Matt 23:37.

2) Resurrection in the OT:
Exod 3:6 (cp. Matt 22:31f); Job 19:25-27; Ps 17:14f; 22:29; 49:14f; Dan 12:2.

3) Jesus spoke Greek:
Matt 4:15; 8:5-13; 13:55; 27:11-14; Mark 2:15; 6:3; 7:25-30; 15:2-5; Luke 5:27; 7:2-10; 23:3; John 4:46-53; 7:35; 12:20-22; 18:33-38.

4) Time of Jesus' earthly life:
5 BC - 30 AD: Matt 2:3-16 (Herod died in Spring 4 BC); Luke 3:1 (Tiberius Caesar's co-reign with Augustus began 11 AD); Luke 3:23 (Jesus about thirty at beginning of ministry); John 2:20 (temple reconstruction began in 19/20 BC); Matt 27:2 (Pilate reigned 26-36 AD); and 3+ year ministry (based on three Passovers attended).

5) The *Imago Dei* (image of God in humans):
Gen 1:26-28 (dominion, communication); Gen 2:16f (moral choices); Gen 2:20 (intelligence, volition); Gen 2:24 (unity in plurality, cp. Deut 6:4); Lev 24:17f,21; Luke 12:7,24 (superior nature of humans over animals) John 1:1; 17:24 (love); Eph 4:24 (righteousness and holiness, cp. Lev 11:44f); Col 3:10 (knowledge); Jam 3:9 (*Imago Dei* still in all people despite the Fall).

6) OT saints filled with the Spirit:
Exod 31:3; 35:31; Numb 27:18; Ezek 2:2; Mic 3:8; Luke 1:67; 1Pet 1:10f.

7) The Kingdom of God:
Matt 6:33; 12:28; 13:24-50; 19:23f; Mark 1:15; 9:1; Luke 17:20f; 19:11-15; John 18:33-37; Col 1:13f; Heb 12:28.

8) Forgiving others:
Matt 6:12-15; 18:21f; Mark 11:25f; Eph 4:31f; Col 3:12f.

9) Submit to God:
Exod 10:3; Deut 8:2-6; 28:1f,15; 2Chr 33:21-24; Mic 6:8; Matt 26:36-44; John 5:30; 6:38; Acts 22:6-10; 2Cor 5:14f; Phil 2:5-8; Jam 4:7-10; 1Pet 5:6.

10) Lordship salvation:
Matt 3:7-10; 7:17-27; Luke 19:11-15; 24:46f; John 3:3-5; 14:15,21-24; 15:1-8; Rom 2:5-11; 6:1-7; 1Cor 6:9-11;

16:22; 2Cor 5:14-21; Gal 5:19-25; Col 2:6; Heb 12:14; 1John 3:9.

Note: All Scripture references from: *The New King James Version*. Nashville, TN: Thomas Nelson Publishers, 1982, unless otherwise indicated.

Appendixes

Appendix #1

Essentials of "The Faith"

Jude exhorts Christians, "... to contend earnestly for the faith which was once for all delivered to the saints" (Jude 3). But what does he mean by "the faith"? In this context, "faith" (Greek-*pistis*) means ". . . the content of what Christians believe--the faith, beliefs, doctrine" (Louw and Nida, Vol. I, p. 379).

So we are talking about beliefs, doctrines. But which ones? Christians have many beliefs about many subjects. Which ones are essential to the Christian faith?

The Unity of the Early Church

In the early Church (the Church of the second and third centuries), these questions were answered by appealing to the "Rule of Faith." Origen (185-254 AD) described the Rule of Faith as follows: "The holy apostles when preaching the faith of Christ, took certain doctrines, those namely which they believed to be the essential ones, and delivered them in the plainest terms to all believers . . ." (Stevenson, p. 198).

Concerning these doctrines, Irenaeus (120-203 AD) wrote:

... the Church, having received this preaching, and this faith, although scattered throughout the whole world, yet, as if occupying but one house carefully preserves it. She also believes these points of doctrine just as if she had but one soul and one and the same heart, and she proclaims

189

them, and teaches them, and hands them down, with perfect harmony, as if she possessed only one mouth. For, although the languages of the world are dissimilar, yet the import of the tradition is one and the same (Stevenson, p. 112).

So there was a unity in the early Church and this unity centered around certain doctrines the apostles had specifically stated were essential to the Christian faith.

The Unity of Today's Church

But what about today? There are hundreds of Christian denominations and associations, along with numerous independent churches. The Christian Church is no longer speaking with "only one mouth"--or is it?

Much time and effort went into drafting Darkness to Light's Confession of Faith (see Appendix #2). The main source used was the Rule of Faith. Also, the writings of the early Church Fathers in general were investigated. In addition, the documents of the early ecumenical councils were studied. Plus, numerous creeds and confessions of various church bodies past and present were compared.

The purpose of all this research was to determine what the major emphases of the Christian Church have been down through the ages. Also, of course, the Scriptures were searched to be sure that all of the points to be included on the confession were strongly Biblical and central teachings of the Word of God (Acts 17:11).

The confession thus represents the doctrines around which true Christians through history and throughout the world today are united (Acts 2:24; Heb 12:1). The Church of today still speaks with "only one mouth" when it teaches, proclaims, and defends these essentials of the Christian faith (1Tim 2:2; Acts 17:22,23; 1Pet 3:15).

Beyond the ten articles on the confession, there are important (though non-essential) doctrines and practices about which Christians disagree. These topics do need to be addressed (Acts 20:27). When discussing such topics, this ministry generally presents a Reformed-Baptist perspective.

But it must be remembered, these areas are secondary topics. One's decision to accept or reject the Christian faith needs to be based on one's attitude towards the essentials of the faith. It is these doctrines which constitute the core of the Christian faith.

In addition, when Christians discuss areas outside of the essentials of the faith they should abide by the attitude of Chrysostom (347-407 AD), "In essentials unity, in non-essentials charity, in all things Jesus Christ" (Prov 18:19; Eph 4:1-3).

Bibliography:

Louw, Johannes P. and Eugene Nida. *Greek-English Lexicon of the New Testament*. New York: United Bible Societies, 1988.

Stevenson, J. A New Eusebius: *Documents Illustrating the History of the Church to AD 337*. Revised by W. H. C. Frend. London: SPCK, 1987.

Appendix #2:

Darkness to Light's Confession of Faith

We Believe:

1) The Holy Scriptures, both Old and New Testaments, to be the inspired Word of God, without error in the original manuscripts, the complete revelation of His will for our salvation and the Divine and final authority for all Christian faith and life.

2) There is one, and only one, true God: Creator and Sustainer of all things, Omnipotent, Omniscient, Omnipresent, Self-existent, Immutable, Spirit, Incomprehensible, Eternal, Sovereign and Master of the universe, infinitely perfect in love, goodness, holiness, and justice.

3) Within the one Being or essence of God, there eternally exists three distinct yet equal Persons, God the Father, God the Son, and God the Holy Spirit.

4) In the full Deity and full humanity of Jesus Christ. These two distinct natures, perfect deity and perfect humanity, are inseparably united in the one Person.

5) In Jesus Christ's virgin birth, sinless life, death on the cross for our sins, burial, bodily resurrection from the dead, ascension into heaven (where at the right hand of God, He is our High Priest, Advocate, Savior, and Lord), and in His visible and bodily return.

193

6) In the full Deity and full personality of the Holy Spirit and in His work in regeneration and sanctification.

7) Human beings were created in the image of God, to glorify God and be in fellowship with Him. We, however, rebelled against Him and are now sinners by nature and by choice. We, therefore, stand condemned before God, deserving of His wrath and are unable to reconcile ourselves to Him by any form or amount of human works, merits, or ceremonies.

8) Salvation comes only by the grace and love of God, through regeneration by the Holy Spirit, repentance of sin, and faith in the Person and work of the Lord Jesus Christ.

9) In the bodily resurrection of the dead, of the believer to everlasting blessedness and joy with the Lord, of the unbeliever to judgment, everlasting conscious torment and separation from God. We further believe in the conscious existence of all souls between death and resurrection, of the believer in heaven with God, of the unbeliever in Hades apart from the Lord.

10) In the existence of angels and Satan and his demons. Angels are personal, spirit beings in the service of God. Satan and his demons are personal, spirit beings who are in rebellion against God, His angels, and His people. Their fate of eternal damnation was sealed by Christ at the cross, and authority over them and their activities has been granted to all believers.

Appendix #3:

About Darkness to Light

Gary F. Zeolla is the founder and director of Darkness to Light ministry. Darkness to Light's Web site is located at: http://www.dtl.org

Darkness to Light 's Web site is dedicated to God Almighty for His use in giving people an understanding of what the Christian faith teaches, and why. It is hoped He will use the site to lead people to realize that a commitment to Jesus Christ and the Christian worldview is intellectually defensible. For those who have already committed their lives to Christ, a better understanding of the teachings of the Christian faith will enable them to, "... grow in the grace and knowledge of our Lord and Savior Jesus Christ" (2 Peter 3:18).

The name for the ministry is taken from the following verse:
"... to open their eyes, in order to turn them from DARKNESS TO LIGHT, and from the power of Satan to God, that they may receive forgiveness of sins and an inheritance among those who are sanctified by faith in [Christ]" (Acts 26:18).

The words "darkness" and "light" have a wide range of meanings when used metaphorically in Scripture. But basically, "darkness" refers to falsehood and unrighteousness while "light" refers to truth and righteousness. People turn from darkness to light when they come to believe the teachings of the Bible and live in accordance with them.

195

"Explaining and Defending the Christian Faith"

Above is the purpose statement for Darkness to Light. Looking at the last phrase first, the Christian faith refers to the essential doctrines of Christianity (Jude 3). Darkness to Light's Confession of Faith lists what this ministry believes are these essential doctrines (see Appendix #2).

As for the first point, there is a great need for the Christian faith to be explained today (Acts 18:26). This is especially true on the Internet where misconceptions abound about what the Christian faith entails. In addition, there are many attacks being made on the Christian faith throughout cyberspace (and in real space). So the Christian faith needs to be defended (1Peter 3:15).

Furthermore, Darkness to Light ministry realizes there is a need to declare, "the whole counsel of God" (Acts 20:27). So there are articles posted on the Web site that address important though non-essential doctrines. When discussing such topics, Darkness to Light generally presents a Reformed-Baptist perspective. But the emphasis is always on explaining and defending the essentials of the Christian faith (1Tim 4:6-16).

Analytical-Literal Translation

Another project this writer is involved in is a new translation of the Bible. It is called the *Analytical-Literal Translation of the Holy Bible*. Scripture verses marked ALT in this book are taken from this new translation.

The ALT is currently in progress and undergoing several stages of production. The ALT adheres to a "literal" or "formal equivalence" method of translating, while "analyzing" details of the vocabulary and grammar of the

Hebrew and Greek texts. In initial stages the New Testament will be based on the *Textus Receptus*. Later, conversion will be made to the *Byzantine Majority Text*.

For further information about the ALT, see the "ALT: Main Page" on Darkness to Light's Web site: http://www.dtl.org/alt/index.html

Contact Information

The author of this book can be contacted at: gary@dtl.org - but please note the following:

1. I generally use my handheld PC to check and answer e-mail. It can only receive "text only" messages. So please do not send me "rich text" or HTML formatted e-mails, or attached files.

2. All e-mails are read and taken under consideration. But I regret I simply do not have the time to respond to everyone personally.

3. E-mails of general interest will be published, edited, and commented upon as I deem appropriate. Published e-mails will only include the e-mailer's first name or initials, unless otherwise requested. If you do not want your e-mail published, write "Confidential" at the top of the message.

4. Comments can also be sent via "snail mail" to: Gary F. Zeolla ~ c/o Darkness to Light ~ PO Box 138 ~ Natrona Heights, PA 15065.

About the Author

Gary F. Zeolla is the founder and director of Darkness to Light ministry - http://www.dtl.org